SKIING |
from the Inside

SKIING

FROM THE INSIDE

The Self-Help Guide to Mastering the Slopes

Sarah Ferguson

SIMON & SCHUSTER
LONDON · SYDNEY · NEW YORK · TOKYO · TORONTO

in association with the Daily Mail

First published in Great Britain by
Simon & Schuster Ltd in 1989

Copyright © Sarah Ferguson, 1989

Simon & Schuster Ltd
West Garden Place
Kendal Street
London W2 2AQ

Simon & Schuster of Australia Pty Ltd
Sydney

British Library Cataloguing-in-Publication Data available
ISBN 0-671-69711-0

Typeset in 10/11pt Palatino by The Picador Group
Printed and bound in Great Britain by
Richard Clay Ltd, Bungay, Suffolk

Contents

Acknowledgements

No book is written in isolation. I have been guided by many people who will see their ideas and experiences reflected in these pages.

John Shedden has been coach and mentor from the beginning, nudging me into all sorts of experiences so that I could make discoveries.

Annie Sarson encouraged me from the very inception of 'The Complete Course in Balance', worked with me on the courses and has contributed her experience as a yoga teacher in chapter seven. My clients have shared their ups and downs with me and from them I have learned to trust the inner coach. *Skiing from the Inside* confirms what they have taught me.

In particular I would like to acknowledge the coaching and friendship given by the following people: Gilly and Craig Adkins, Graham and Anita Alexander, Christine Baxter-Jones, Dennis Edwards, John Falkiner, Alan Fine, Dave Francis, Tim Gallwey, Jerry Harnett, Fred Harper, Alan Hughes, Bob Kriegel, Peter Kronig, Edwina and Peter Lightfoot, Tom McNab, Suzie Morel, the Morgan family, Julie Norman, Alan Quinn, Ali Ross, Mark Shapiro, Julia Strange, Roger and Beryl Turner, Colin Whiteside and John and Diana Whitmore.

The list of skiing friends who have inspired me during the past sixteen years is far too long to include. If we had fun skiing together, you are on it!

Certain organizations have contributed a great deal to my education as a coach: the English Ski Council, the British Association of National Coaches, the National Coaching Foundation, and Results Unlimited.

Ian McMillan encouraged me to write and published the series 'On Balance' in the magazine *Skiing UK*. The initial idea for this book originated in that series and excerpts from those articles have found their way into these pages.

Several people in the equipment business have given all sorts of support over the years. I have tested and trusted their products in every condition imaginable, and their generosity is greatly appreciated.

Klaus Brandstätter - Atomic Skis
Kim and Fiona Smith-Bingham - Schöffel Clothing
Eric Bean - Panasonic UK
Oliver Hart - Salomon Ski Bindings
Tim Meyer - Lange Boots (Kent Shuss)
Walter Hughes - Hestra Gloves

A very special thank you to Robbie Robinson for encouraging me and for making the teaching principles outlined in this book available through the Daily Mail National Ski Courses.

Lastly, my family, whose love and support have given me the impetus and courage to follow my instinct.

The 'mind maps' at the beginning of each chapter were inspired by Tony Buzan in his book *Use Your Head*.

This book is dedicated to Swami Chidvilasananda (Gurumayi) with gratitude for her grace.

For further information about the
COMPLETE COURSE IN BALANCE contact:

Made to Measure Holidays Limited
43 East Street
Chichester
West Sussex PO19 1HX
Tel: Chichester (0243) 533333

Glossary of skiing terms

ANGULATION   The dynamic active balancing posture which assists refined edge control. The upper body is flexed forwards at the hips and the legs rotate in the pelvis to steer the skis.

AERIAL EVENT   One of the events of freestyle skiing where the skier performs a jump and is judged for height, style and precision on landing.

BALLET EVENT   One of the events of freestyle skiing where spins, steps and jumps are choreographed to music. Points are awarded for technical difficulty, choreography and overall performance.

EDGING   The lateral tilt of the skis towards the slope to control sideways movement.

FALL-LINE   The imaginary line that follows the most direct (steepest) route down a hillside.

FLOW-LINE   The imaginary line a skier's centre of mass takes whilst in motion.

FREESTYLE   One of the disciplines of alpine skiing involving three events: ballet, moguls and aerials.

MOGULS   Round or oblong bumps caused by erosion as skiers turn in the same place in soft snow.

MOGUL EVENT   One of the events of freestyle skiing which

entails fall-line skiing in steep moguls. The skier is judged on the quality and quantity of their turns, speed and jumping skill. Only upright jumps are permitted.

OFF PISTE	Unmarked, unprepared, unpatrolled terrain.
PISTE	A marked, groomed ski run where hazards and injured skiers are taken care of by the ski patrol. They are classified according to difficulty as green (easiest), blue, red and black.
PLOUGHING	Skiing with the skis in a snowplough shape. Ploughing can be either a braking manoeuvre or a means to steer the skis.
POWDER	A term used to describe fresh snow, untouched by skiers or piste machines.
SKIDDING	A sideways movement of the skis after they have been turned across the skier's direction of momentum.
SNOWPLOUGH	Basic skiing posture where the tails of the skis are pushed out to form a 'V' shape.
SNOW SNAKE	A mythical creature that wraps its tentacles around the ankles and causes the skier to fall. Otherwise known as an excuse.
STEERING	Changing direction as a result of pressure applied against a ski when it is edged and turned at an angle to its motion.
STEM	The action of moving one ski at an angle to the other.
T-BAR	A ski tow that pulls skiers uphill in pairs.

Introduction

When competing in the 1970's I was involved in a branch of skiing called freestyle, which at that time had not been recognized within the family of skiing. Without the backing of a national governing body we were on our own. I longed for a coach to guide me, to support my development and to help me overcome the internal and external obstacles that interfere with learning and enjoyment.

Even though my circumstances were extreme, it struck me that many people have this need. Some recreational skiers are lucky enough to have formed an on-going relationship with an expert who guides their progress over the years. Unfortunately, the majority of skiers are on their own in the skiing jungle, learning by trial and error with irregular input from a variety of sources– ski school instructors, friends and books.

My intention in *Skiing from the Inside* is to create a context for skiers to help themselves through the ups and downs of learning to ski and to maximize their potential on the slopes. It is not intended to replace coaching or instruction but to blend with them so that you can master both skiing and learning. To this end there is something for everybody. If you are a beginner you may find that some of the more technical explanations in chapter three do not connect with your current understanding so you can skip these until they make more sense. Likewise, some of the basic advice may seem obvious if you have already gained some skiing experience.

HOW TO USE THIS BOOK

Skiing from the Inside is a type of 'workbook' which presents opportunities for participation to help you to become more aware of your body, mind and emotions. There are several exercises which can be done at home to accelerate progress once on the slopes. To get the most out of the exercises you will need a notebook to record and clarify your responses. In this way you will begin to understand and take greater responsibility for your learning.

The 'mind maps' at the beginning of each chapter are designed to give you an overview of the subject and to make logical connections between the material presented.

Ideally you will make friends with this book and realize that whatever your aspirations you can refer to the exercises again and again to guide and support your learning and enjoyment.

Chapter One

From agony to ecstasy

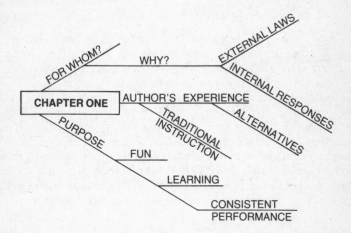

It is fifteen years since I began learning to ski, and during all that time I have consistently experienced both the agony and the ecstasy of the sport of skiing. This has led me to conclude that the highs and lows, the joys and frustrations, of this marvellous sport are a common feature at every level of skill.

Whether a beginner on the gentlest nursery slope or an expert on the steepest black run, the problems that we experience are essentially the same: tension, anxiety, awkwardness, loss of concentration or even the boredom of being stuck on a 'learning plateau'. These states may manifest externally in different ways, but we experience them internally and can trace their origins either to misperception or to misunderstanding the workings of our minds, our bodies or the laws that we are automatically subjected to when we don a pair of skis.

Yet most traditional teaching techniques seem to present the sport in a very complicated, fragmented way that misses the essence of what skiing is. Too little advice is given on how we can minimise the agony by seeing every part of the learning process in the context of the whole.

Whenever I ask my clients what they would like from their skiing, their responses can always be categorized under three headings.

- LEARNING
- CONSISTENT PERFORMANCE
- FUN/ENJOYMENT

They want to **learn** – by improving their skiing, by overcoming anxiety or about learning itself. They want to **perform** what they already know with greater consistency, and, most importantly, they want to **have fun** in the process.

You may be fearful or you may wish to improve your style. Or perhaps you are simply confused by jargon and different techniques. Whatever you want from skiing, this book will give you the key to self-coaching. Use it to take charge of your learning process or to support a child or a partner with theirs. *Skiing from the Inside* is for people who want to discover more of their potential and to overcome the obstacles that inhibit learning, performing and enjoying this wonderful sport.

DANCING WITH A MOUNTAIN

Skiing is like a complex dance with one partner, the mountain. The dance can be a slow smooch, a graceful waltz or a vibrant tango. We can choose the pace and tempo that suits us but our partner remains in charge, oblivious to our strengths and weaknesses but with an uncanny habit of pointing them out. Skiing is like looking in a mirror: the reflection is always truthful but the interpretation of the image our personal affair. The way we approach our relationship with this uncompromising dance partner will ultimately determine how much satisfaction we get out of skiing. It may figure as a small part of most people's existence - for two weeks in every fifty-two for the majority of participants - but somehow its appeal and most certainly its many rewards make it well worth spending time and effort to do it well.

If my own experience is anything to go by, simply being in the mountains, breathing the fresh, clean air and seeing a vast expanse of comparative wilderness recharges my batteries and energises me. Feeling comfortable within this environment and using it as my playground is something I want to share with others. *Skiing from the Inside* will hopefully help you to deepen your understanding of yourself in relation to this magnificent, beautiful and demanding dance partner.

LEARNING AS AN ADULT

Unlike most ski teachers, I did not learn to ski as a child. After an unsuccessful attempt at the age of 9 I did not return to the slopes until I was 23.

I imagine that the majority of people who pick up this book will also be adults. The natural learners amongst us – the children who zip past, leaving us amazed by the speed at which they learn, their fearlessness, their fun and laughter – are unlikely to be interested.

When starting again from scratch, it was not fear that blocked my enjoyment and learning but confusion. So many different instructions about where my limbs ought to be and weren't. So much criticism and focus upon what I was not doing right and what I *should* be doing. Feeling like a square peg in a round hole, I instinctively eschewed ski school and began following friends, having fun, falling over, laughing and copying anyone whose rhythm and grace caught my eye. As someone who has survived the spectrum of adult teaching and learning styles, perhaps I can relate to you and your skiing in a way that many ski instructors who learned naturally as children cannot.

Fortunately, fear was something I did not experience as a learner or I might never have got as far as I did so quickly. In my teens I had learned to fall off a galloping horse so falling off a pair of skis was 'no big deal'; in fact, it seemed huge fun to roll around in the snow after mud, gorse bushes and frozen ground.

It was later on in my skiing career, as an international freestyle competitor, that I first experienced fear. Nervousness and anxiety were tolerable but not the overwhelming sense of panic that developed after an injury. I lost my nerve, the joy of skiing vanished and a sense of dread at the thought of even an intermediate slope overwhelmed me.

There is no doubt that fear is the single most inhibiting factor in any activity, and in skiing it seems to be the most commonly expressed obstacle. I have not encountered many skiers who do not at some point experience anxiety. With a trained eye it is not difficult to recognize that most skiers on a slope express some level of tension in their bodies, whether they admit to it or not. Having confronted the problem of fear myself, I have great respect for anyone who is in the same situation and still willing to carry on. I am amazed that there has been so little written on the subject, at most half a page, and that it seems so little understood. Of course, not everyone experiences extreme fear, but, in understanding its dynamics, even those occasional anxious moments can be minimised.

Fortunately John Shedden (Director of Coaching for the English Ski Council) suggested I attend the first European course of Tim Gallwey's 'Inner Game'. This teaching method focuses on overcoming the internal obstacles that inhibit learning and enjoyment. There I discovered that I actually had a choice about how I felt and my love of skiing quickly returned with improved performance and a greater sense of inspiration. I have always been intrigued by what makes people tick – or not tick as the case tends to be. Fascinated by my own changed attitude, I pursued this interest in how we can overcome obstacles and unlock our personal best by becoming an 'Inner Skiing' and 'Inner Tennis' coach.

A COMPLETE COURSE IN BALANCE

After leading 'Inner Skiing' courses in Europe from 1979-82 and coaching the English and British freestyle teams for a couple of years, I set up my own ski course in 1985 to offer the recreational skier personal coaching. The course included the aspects of the Inner Game that I had found so helpful as well as an exercise programme to develop a more balanced body structure and to improve physical fitness. I had noticed that even when someone overcame the inner obstacles to learning, progress was often inhibited by poor posture, physical imbalance or lack of sensitivity – a case of the spirit being willing and the flesh being weak.

To make the course 'complete' I felt that an understanding of the laws of motion and how we balance would clarify many confusions about technique. All commercial ski schools have expressed their analyses of how to ski in different ways, causing frustration for holiday makers who are told that what they paid for last year is not 'right' and must be done 'like this'. Similarly many ski instruction books are full of detailed analyses of a variety of techniques. Crammed with what you should or should not do, they boggle the mind with detail. Never mind that you may not be able to translate these words into actions or that the technique being propounded does not actually tally with the laws of motion.

It seems we have made numerous intellectual assaults on skiing without ever recognising what the real role of the mind is. We need to honour the crucial part that the intellect plays and learn how to direct it in ways that assist us. Some knowledge of how the mind itself works, an understanding of the physical forces that affect us, and the capabilities of the equipment we use, are all part of becoming a complete skier.

My purpose in writing this book it to share my Complete Course in Balance with a wider public and to provide a clear and practical guide to learning about learning and about *Skiing from the Inside*.

HOW TO GET THE MOST OUT OF THIS BOOK

Someone who has skied for years will experience this book in a different way from someone who has just begun the sport. The beginner who has fewer preconceptions and less knowledge may actually find the content easier to grasp than someone steeped in traditional methodology and mythology. Either way, what is important is what you experience as you discover how to express yourself through the sport. When Michelangelo was asked what he was doing chipping away at a block of marble, he said that there was an angel in there waiting to be discovered. Likewise there is a skier in you waiting to emerge who will exceed your expectations, given half a chance.

You may find *Skiing from the Inside* uncomfortably different.

Instead of breaking down patterns of movement into separate stages and instructing you how to rebuild them I will be asking questions designed to direct your attention so that you can discover what works for you. **If this is to happen, you will have to participate. In order to uncover the elusive talent that you possess, that of learning, or to become more consistent in performing what you already know and get maximum enjoyment, you have to get in touch with what is true for you, to gain access to your own experience.**

You can read this book from cover to cover and not participate in the exercises. If you do, you will get some interesting insights into how human beings function but make relatively little progress yourself. If you want to express more of your potential as a skier, I encourage you to put as much as you can into the exercises. There is nothing in this book that you cannot do, no risk to life or limb, and your willingness to play along will pay dividends in the end.

I also ask you to withhold judgement as you read about whether the process is working or not. Many things may not make sense at first, and if you are continually looking for results you may miss the point completely. Please trust the process: you can make judgements later on if you still want to.

COACHING NOT INSTRUCTION

The process you are embarked upon is one of 'self-coaching' rather than 'self-instructing'. To understand the distinction you need to understand the way our brains function. When I encountered the Inner Game in 1978 I had initially to take on trust its principles until my own experience demonstrated their validity. Since then, research into how the brain functions has provided us with scientific evidence that these principles are sound so I have included facts that will help enrol you in this voyage of self-discovery.

As you become your own coach, the distinction between the words 'instructor' and 'coach' will become clear. At this stage it can be best explained by the old proverb, 'Give a man a fish and you feed him for a day. Teach him how to fish and you feed him for life.'

Instructors feed you with fishes, coaches with the art of fishing. This does not mean that you will never want or need to take another lesson or read another book. It does mean that you can take charge of your learning and will be able to interpret instructions in a way that really works for you.

We are used to thinking that the answers lie outside us and that teachers can provide them. With this expectation we are naturally frustrated when the instructor tells us what to do and we either do not understand or cannot do it with any regularity. There seems to be a link missing between the intention and the action. It is this link that we will be exploring together so that you can interpret technical instructions in a way that makes sense.

LEARNING IS OUR BIRTHRIGHT

> *Learning is finding out what you already know.*
>
> *Doing is demonstrating that you know it.*
>
> *Teaching is reminding others that they know just as well as you.*
>
> *You are all learners, doers, teachers.*
>
> Richard Bach (*Illusions*)

Most of my experiences with traditional teaching methods left me feeling frustrated and confused. If I had to choose just one thing that I would like you to get out of this book, it would be the belief that learning can be effortless and enormous fun.

Learning is our birthright and does not require struggle and effort.

Unfortunately, the communication medium of a book does not allow me to get to know you personally and respond to your particular needs. However, thanks to the many clients from whose experiences I have learned a great deal, I trust in your innate wisdom and creative learning capabilities. You may be partially out of touch with them now, but rest assured that you will have a box of useful tools and a different perspective by the time we are through!

In the words of William Blake, *Great things are done when men and mountains meet.*

Chapter Two

Balancing and the brain

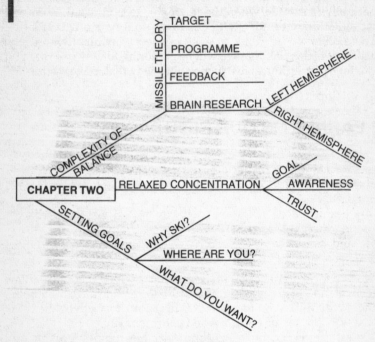

STAYING ON YOUR FEET

Skiing is all about staying on your feet. André Gide said, 'A state of balance is attractive only when one is on a tightrope; seated on the ground, there is nothing wonderful about it.' Yet from that familiar seated position on the slopes a skier might well consider a state of balance something wonderful. Certainly we take our everyday ability to balance for granted – until we lose it.

Standing upright requires an incredibly complex interplay of senses and muscles; add to that some movement like walking or running and it becomes staggeringly complicated. Dancing or playing games like tennis or badminton require fast changes of direction in exact response to external stimuli. Skiing stretches our ability to balance even further by increasing the length of the feet fivefold, and replacing the familiar friction underfoot with a surface which is slippery *and* sloping.

Balancing is a reflex action. It is performed without our conscious control and, like any computing machine, the quality and quantity of input will influence the quality and variety of output, a process once graphically referred to as 'garbage in, garbage out'.

When in a receptive state, apart from the more obvious visual and auditory detail of our whereabouts, a multitude of sensory nerve endings in our skin, muscles, tendons, joints and ears provide input for our overall kinaesthetic perception, our 'sense' of balance and movement. This information is processed by the nervous system (in relation to the goal set by the conscious mind) and the body activates and relaxes a myriad of muscle fibres to stay erect. (It may help to compare those muscle fibres to the guy ropes on a tent.) All this happens in fractions of a second. We can tell the body what to do, but to think that we can tell it *how* to do it is laughable.

As adults we all possess a vast amount of unacknowledged experience of balancing in a variety of activities. Skiing poses new and somewhat different challenges but we already have many resources to call upon – if we allow ourselves.

Please stand up for a moment and become aware of your feet. Can you notice the different muscles working? If you stand on one foot, you will observe how the body takes care of balancing. You may find balancing on one foot difficult and, as you lose equilibrium, your other foot will instantly come to the rescue to save you from toppling over.

It is very difficult to gain conscious access to this non-verbal, silent knowledge. In fact as soon as we start to 'instruct' ourselves to stay on our feet we tend to become less balanced rather than more so. Paradoxically, trying not to fall only produces unwanted tension which inhibits the muscles' responses and so creates a greater likelihood of falling. How many times have you seen someone put the right leg and hand forward when 'thinking about' marching? But if that same person marched without thinking, he or she would unhesitatingly use alternate arms and legs. Similarly, trying hard to get to sleep usually guarantees wakefulness!

THE 'MISSILE' THEORY

Did you ever marvel at how clever your body is? It is programmed to raise the alarm when it lacks air, food or water. It converts food to a usable energy source, stores it and then controls its expenditure, processes the waste, controls the sewage system, regulates the heating and drainage systems and adapts to all sorts of demands. The human body is an information processor with capabilities of self regulation in respect of an overall goal. Each cell of the human body is programmed and operates on the same principle as a missile or a thermostat. Once you have set the target temperature on a thermostat, its regulator reads the ambient air temperature and automatically switches on and off as appropriate. Similarly, a missile reaches its destination by receiving feedback about its whereabouts in relation to the target.

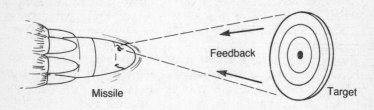

Fig. 2.1

Now if the whole human organism responds to such principles, and our intention is to learn to ski, given that we trust that the organism is preprogrammed to adapt to demands put upon it, all we need to do is to maximize the input and feedback both during and after the activity in relation to the target; the body will take care of the rest. It follows, of course, that our goals must be realistic and specific and our bodies must be given the freedom to do what they know best with minimum interference.

Cyberneticists (those who study control and communication in the animal and the machine) use a deceptively simple statement that we can apply to any activity in order to achieve results: 'It is the target itself which controls performance.' If I want to make a telephone call at 3.15pm (target) and it is now 3.00pm (where I am in relation to the target), by maintaining my awareness of the time (now) I can be accurate to the second. It is this awareness of where we are now that steers us automatically towards a specific goal.

TRUST

Trusting our ability to adapt and learn is the way to express our potential. To do this we need to understand more about our behaviour and how we inhibit this seemingly simple process.

THE OUTER AND INNER GAMES

Tim Gallwey, the author of *The Inner Game of Tennis*, points out that there are two games that we play in life. The outer game can be anything – a sport like tennis or skiing or an activity like playing the piano or driving the car. Whether we get to express our potential in the outer game, depends on how we play the inner game. The inner game is what goes on internally, the way we react to the situations that confront us. It involves our motivation, clarity and confidence and how we confront issues like self-doubt, fear, boredom, lack of concentration or lack of direction.

The importance of the inner game is often clearly demonstrated to us by top-level tennis or golf competition. Both players may have different strengths and weaknesses but after a couple of hours the score is virtually even. The one who wins is usually the one whose inner game is stronger: the one who keeps cool in spite of the pressure, the one who conserves energy, the one who maintains focus like a Zen master.

Let's make this a little more real for you by getting in touch with your own inner game.

From one extreme . . .

What I'd like you to do is to recall your favourite memory on skis, a time when everything clicked. Take a few moments to cast your mind back.

What was it like? Re-create as much of the scenario as you can. It may have been fleeting – a few turns that felt effortless and flowing or several descents when you plugged into a rhythm never experienced before. How did your body feel? What was going on in your mind? What were you feeling? It is worth jotting down the first words that come to mind so that you can keep them for future comparison.

If you have not done much skiing or have been unlucky enough to have had nothing but traumatic skiing experiences and cannot recall any pleasant moments, recall your best moment in another physical activity.

Many people find it hard to recall what was happening in these special moments apart from feelings of exhilaration and effortlessness. Even so they stay in our minds and are one of the reasons why we keep returning to the slopes. One of my first experiences of this nature is as clear as if it happened yesterday. I can recall a feeling in my tummy of being completely balanced, connected with the planet, and of my feet knowing exactly where to go. It was as if I had become a part of the mountain and knew its secrets. After a while a voice spoke in my head, 'Aha, so this is it!' and the spell was broken.

. . . to another

Now recall your most painful moment on skis or if you have never had one, recall your worst moment in another physical activity. How did your body feel and what was going on in your head? Jot down some of the words that come into your mind.

You probably have a vivid picture in your mind. I certainly do. It was a red run called 'Paradise' which sounded easy enough. It was, in fact, well within my capabilities but 'Paradise' did not live up to its name – it turned out to be purgatory.

Just to be sure that I did not fall, I began to repeat all the instructions that I had first heard at the age of 9.

> Mountain shoulder forward, weight on the lower ski. No, not like that – more weight on the lower ski. Watch out, you are going too fast! Slow down, you have to turn at the end. No, I can't turn here. Don't be stupid, Sarah. You'll only fall in that deep snow over there. You see, I told you so. Now why can't you do as I say? Pull yourself together. Remember to bend your knees. . .'

As I tried harder to follow the instructions I was giving myself, the tension increased in my body and I fell more and more frequently. My breathing was short and gasping and I began to have visions of being there all night. The slope seemed to get steeper and steeper. It was as if I had forgotten everything I thought I knew about skiing. Needless to say I made it down, exhausted and frustrated.

The difference

It may be useful for you to compare the words that you jotted down with my lists:

THE ECSTASY	THE AGONY
Exhilarated	Frightened
Flowing	Tense
Effortless	Confused
Easy	Exhausted
Fun	Frustrated
Rhythmical	Jerky
Balanced	Uncoordinated
Connected	Clumsy
Content	Angry
Centred	Defensive
Light	Heavy

You can learn a great deal about your inner game by comparing these two extremes. To hazard a guess, it is likely that in the ecstatic moment your mind was serene and that in the agonizing moment you experienced a lot of 'mental chatter'. This is the root of the problem encountered in those agonizing moments – the mind thinks it is doing the skiing. It gives many instructions and criticisms to the body and wants to control the show.

UNDERSTANDING THE MIND

The problem with understanding the mind is that it is only accessible by thinking and therefore we can never get a completely objective picture of its activity. It is rather like wanting to do a survey on a house and being allowed access only to its interior. We are unable to put into perspective where we are in relation to the rest of the street or to its less immediate surroundings. Stuck inside the house, we might even believe that it is the only property on the street or that we are the rulers of a kingdom.

It is important that I clarify my definitions of certain words before going any further.

Awareness Every living being experiences a degree of consciousness, an awareness of being. Awareness is perceived by the senses rather than the mind and knows no limits. You are probably familiar with that marvellous sense of being at one with your surroundings or loved ones. There is a feeling of completeness, a joy in being alive. We only become conscious of this awareness when the mind is silent. In the spaces between thoughts the awareness behind the mind can watch the mind in motion and observe the flow of thoughts.

Thinking 'Thinking' describes the verbal constructs that the mind makes when analsing, judging, rationalizing, instructing or having opinions. This stream of thoughts, usually random and uncontrolled, includes fears, regrets, expectations and concerns. Verbal thinking is only one aspect of consciousness. Setting goals and making decisions are mental activities which require thought. This sort of verbal mental activity, when done consciously, is essential in skiing but there is an appropriate time and place for it.

Concentration Many people confuse concentration with

'thinking', believing it is something that requires effort. To concentrate means to be 'centred' within physical, emotional and mental balance. When we concentrate, we behave as if the activity has drawn us into itself. Our senses are alert and yet focused. We are capable of absorbing information on several different levels simultaneously. There is no effort, no trying hard, little or no self-talk. We are in a passive, relaxed, receptive state.

You may have a hobby or recreational activity that creates this type of response in you, often leaving you with a feeling of being refreshed. It is the state in which our goal is clearly envisaged, in which we have confidence and trust in our abilities, when learning takes place, when we perform at our best and usually experience the most enjoyment.

Feedback Feedback is the information that we glean, consciously or unconsciously, from our actions. It is the knowledge of the results of our actions, from both external and internal sources. Our senses pick up all sorts of information (input), we respond to that input and 'feedback' is what we get as a consequence of our response. Many people wrongly interpret feedback as simple responses of 'right' or 'wrong'. 'I did it wrong' or 'That ski turn was a load of rubbish' is not useful feedback because it does not tell us anything about what really happened. Every experience can provide valuable feedback, whether it appears to be a 'load of rubbish' or not. By putting a value judgement on what we do, we actually deny our bodies access to accurate, useful feedback. If all the missile got as feedback was 'wrong, wrong, wrong!', it would not have much information to go on to correct its flight path.

Think about your reaction to a fall, for example. Falling over is the quintessential indication that whatever it was we did, did not work. By getting annoyed and self-critical or ignoring what led up to the fall we rob our processing department of what it needs to know to self-correct the next time it is in a similar situation. Both reasons why we tend to repeat the same mistakes and groove in inefficient, habitual patterns of movement. For feedback to be usefully assimilated we need to delve deeper into our experience and remain detached about what we discover.

ALTERED STATES

When I began to practise non-judgemental awareness while skiing I started to experience time and speed in a different way. My mind would become immersed in the game and my perceptions would alter, giving me a feeling of being connected to the mountain as if it were part of me. As my awareness expanded, time seemed to slow down and although skiing fast there was never any sense of rush or speed; I would feel as if I was moving in slow motion and whoever was doing the moving knew a lot more about skiing than I did. Fascinated by these discoveries, I started to enquire into what was going on by reading books and asking questions. Altered states of perception seemed so shrouded in mystery, so foreign and like so many things that we don't understand often give a wide berth in conversation. As Carlos Castaneda said in *The Power of Silence:*

> *Heightened awareness is a mystery only for our reason. In practice it is very simple. As with everything else we complicate matters by trying to make the immensity that surrounds us reasonable.*

Any process of sustained mental attention or concentration can be called meditation. This word had connotations of lotus posture, navels and austerity, so I never associated it with an activity like skiing. To many people, anything that cannot be understood by the mind and put into a tidy little box or concept is considered weird and to be avoided at all costs. From the experiences I was having on skis, all I could say was that I was skiing 'out of my mind' so neither my mind nor anyone else's was capable of understanding this experience. There were times when the skiing would be happening and I would be merely an observer watching my body make all the appropriate movements and responses - even adapting to and coping with situations that my mind would not have conceived to have been within my abilities. In this state of 'meditation in action' there is serenity, abundant energy, lightness, clarity and joy. It is as if this is our natural state and that all mental activity is an illusion, a veil over reality.

THE SABOTEUR

The enemy of relaxed concentration and sensory awareness is the mind, the voice in the head, even if it is only whispering. When there is no separation between us and the experience, we are in the present. Mental chatter takes us out of direct experience and either into the past or the future with its concepts, opinions, instructions and judgements. There is nothing 'bad' about this mental activity: it simply takes us away from our awareness of what *is*. When there is true awareness, the entire organism is sensitive, there is mental clarity and intuition.

Thoughts may come and go but the attention is not distracted from what is happening. It is worth getting to know your brand of self-chatter so that you can begin to identify its style of interference.

You may notice it chipping in as you read. Voicing opinions about this and that, telling you what you need to do next and generally side-tracking you from the task in hand, that of reading. So who is it talking to? You must be talking to yourself since there is no external audience listening in. Tim Gallwey uses a useful model to express these two functional aspects of the mind. He calls the voice 'Self 1' and the part of us that it is talking to, the doer, 'Self 2 '. When Self 2 is allowed to express itself while we are skiing and the voice is quiet, we free our bodies and perform 'out of our minds' as in our 'ecstatic moment'. *Getting to know these dramatically different parts of ourselves, developing their strengths and learning to harmonize their activities is the key to self-coaching and unlocking our potential as skiers.*

FROM INTUITION TO FACT

Scientists and philosophers have still only scratched the surface of understanding how the human brain functions, although during the past fifteen years there have been more discoveries than in the previous fifty. But the more we find out the more we realize we do not know. Our perceptions of our capabilities are altering and changes in educational methods are emerging as these discoveries become common knowledge.

In the 1970's when Tim Gallwey 'developed' the Inner Game

he based his theories upon his own observation and intuition. Since then a Nobel Prize has been awarded to Dr Roger Sperry of the California Institute of Technology for his research into brain hemisphere functioning. Thanks to Sperry and his colleagues we can now take a look at Gallwey's model of Self 1 and Self 2 from a more scientific standpoint.

Our brain (cerebral cortex) is in fact a dual organ, consisting of two identical-looking hemispheres joined by a thick bundle of nerve fibres called the *corpus callosum*. Studies of people who suffered damage to one of the hemispheres indicated that the left hemisphere controls the right visual field and the right side of the body and the right hemisphere controls the left visual field and the left side of the body. Thanks to Dr Sperry's famous split-brain experiments and Robert Ornstein's research as a psychologist, it is now proven that these two brains function in fundamentally different ways, sometimes know as convergent cognitive (left hemisphere) and divergent cognitive (right hemisphere) styles.

In the majority of people, the left hemisphere is the home of speech and verbal thinking. We use this hemisphere to verify through logic, understand reality through a linear time record and remember names and numbers.

The right hemisphere knows no time but understands spatial relationships, motion and emotion. This is the part of us that dances, sings, laughs and cries. It is believed to have a direct link with our unconscious and autonomic (automatic) nervous system, receiving information simultaneously in sensory images through touch, smell, sound and sight to create our overall kinaesthetic perception. Its memory is visual (remembers faces) and holistic (multi-dimensional) and it can generate ideas and solve problems through the use of creative imagination. This part of us is so clever that it is impossible for our verbal, sequential mind to understand – given its particular style of functioning and verbal limitations.

Generally speaking the brain's functions are as follows:

LEFT HEMISPHERE	RIGHT HEMISPHERE
Verbal	Visual
Linear	Spatial
Mathematical	Rhythmical
Rational	Intuitive
Logical	Imaginative
Analytical	Multi-dimensional

Decisive	Creative
Sequential	Emotional
Words of a song	Tune of a song

These positive functions of the two hemispheres are counterbalanced by some negative tendencies:

Chattering mind	Imagining the worst
Over-analysis	Daydreaming
Insensitivity	Indecisiveness

However, this seeming separation in functioning is never a complete division of labour. In speech, for instance, the words are generated in the left hemisphere whereas the tone, expression and body language that accompany the words are generated in the right hemisphere. In recognizing the face of a friend, the right hemisphere sees all the features and the left hemisphere remembers the name. Just moving around your home, the decision to go from one room to another may result from logical reasoning but the understanding of where one room is in relation to another comes from that silent partner in the other hemisphere. In reading, the left hemisphere understands the literal interpretation of words and the right hemisphere grasps the whole meaning, including humour, analogies and metaphors.

Choosing your ski resort, rationalizing the expenditure, chatting up the tour representative and deciding which slope best suits you are all left-hemisphere functions. But if you look at the above lists it becomes obvious that the right hemisphere is the one that needs to predominate when actually skiing.

This division of labour is not an either/or, black and white split. The two hemispheres have a symbiotic, synergistic relationship. Like any good partnership there is always some contribution, albeit not obvious, from the other half. The game is to get the appropriate part to function in order to redress any imbalance. In the case of most Western adults this means to acknowledge the role of the right hemisphere, increase sensitivity and allow the skier within greater freedom of expression.

If we are to remain in perfect balance over our skis and respond to everchanging conditions, we need to allow our bodies the maximum possible feedback from our environment.

Understanding slope angles and the spatial relationships between our body and the mountain is a task of enormous complexity which our verbal mind cannot begin to compute. It seems that the more we think the less we sense/feel. Someone once said to me, 'When involved in any action, lose your mind and come to your senses.' That is not a licence to be mindless. **The mind must be allowed to do what it is good at – making decisions, planning, focusing the attention and enhancing through words the work of the silent partner.** In effect what we need to develop is the ability to be 'whole-brained' rather than half-brained.

The stumbling block – as adults brought up in a predominantly 'left-brain' world – is that we tend to apply logical thinking to everything we do. Our left hemisphere has been well educated but our right hemisphere is virtually ignored. Without a voice, the silent partner does not have the ability to argue its case. One of the reasons why children learn so effortlessly is that they have not yet learned to cogitate, or theorize. They are open to experiencing their environment without the need for much self-talk. An error is just feedback that what they did did not work, a chance to have another go and not an opportunity to analyse, judge and self-instruct. Adults inhibit the learning process by creating expectations, harping on memories of failure, having opinions and making judgements.

Children, who have yet to develop their conceptual, intellectual thinking, are the experts when it comes to right-brain activities. However, they need to develop their logical reasoning in order to be able to adapt to the world and to manipulate their environment. Until that happens they need adult guidance to stay safe in the mountains.

THE MISSING LINK

In chapter one I referred to the missing link between intention and action. You may by now have an inkling of its cause. Living in a predominantly left-brain world, reading books and listening to verbal instructions may provide us with a great many facts about skiing. The problem is how to convert these complex concepts into actions! Our bodies do not understand English,

French or Italian so the verbal instructions that we bombard ourselves with are falling on deaf ears.

The body understands only direct experience received via the senses and relates to a multi-dimensional world. Our links with our bodies are through our imaginations in the form of images, pictures, rhythm and feelings. The tune of the song rather than the words. What we need to relearn is body sensitivity, non-verbal right-hemisphere awareness and how to use our imaginations in a creative way. Some people are lucky enough to have retained the link and they can automatically translate words into sensory images or feelings that the body can relate to. These people are the ones whom we might label 'natural athletes'. Surprisingly enough, there is a natural skier waiting to be discovered in you too!

THE TALE OF THE MAGIC WAND

Some years ago, while preparing for one of my ski-instructor qualifications, my trainer pointed out that I was doing several things that I should not be doing. With the examination looming up, it was important to me to get everything right, but, as I attempted to correct these 'faults', my body became more and more tense. In trying to change one thing, another would be forgotten and so on. With the best of intentions, the trainer kept up a steady barrage of criticism, telling me what I was doing wrong and to think of this and think of that. My skiing became more and more unnatural and forced.

One particular instruction was to stop shuffling my feet. Apparently I was unnecessarily sliding my feet, pushing one ski ahead of the other at the start of each turn. In desperation I asked him how I could get rid of this 'bad habit'. He looked at me as if I was Oliver Twist and replied, 'I can tell you what you are doing wrong, and what you should do but I haven't got a magic wand.' I was stunned. Here I was learning how to teach skiing and my trainer was not able to teach me how we learn. How I passed the exam, feeling like a stuffed mechanical parrot with my feet jammed together, I'll never know. Perhaps everybody looked the same!

Shortly after this I attended an Inner Skiing course. My coach,

Peter Kronig, asked me to feel my feet. It was as if the sun came out from behind a dark cloud. 'Feel my feet?' I questioned. 'Yes, feel where the pressure is on the soles of your feet.' Skiing down the slope while aware of my feet I started to notice the changes in pressure and subtle differences of snow texture. There was a huge smile on my face and my mind was quiet. All the instructions that had been going round and round my head had disappeared as had the overriding concern about doing it 'right'. My feet had become alive and responsive again. It was like reaching dry land after a stormy voyage.

The next exercise Peter asked me to do was to notice the relationship between my feet by observing the distance between them and calling out in inches what was *actually happening* without having any concept of what was right or wrong or attempting to change anything. It wasn't long before I became aware of one foot sliding forwards on every turn. I heard the echo of an Austrian instructor yelling 'mountain ski forwards!' and a different voice saying 'don't shuffle your feet'. Focusing back on the awareness exercise so as not to lose the sensation, the shuffling became intermittent and then eventually vanished. By simply paying attention to what was actually happening and feeling the excessive muscle activity my body simplified and smoothed out that superfluous movement.

For me this was a revelation. I realized that *awareness produces change*.

Having tussled so long and hard with this habit, it was more than a relief to find such a simple solution. I was excited, not about my feet but about the process that had revealed itself. I had found the magic wand: the body learns through focused attention, pure observation and feeling rather than verbal instructions.

DEVELOPING AWARENESS

We all know how to concentrate – nothing would get done if we didn't. Even simple actions require focus but to maintain this focus when there is internal chatter or external interference requires skill. Needless to say it takes practice but you can start training before you next go skiing so that once on the slopes you are familiar with the process. The stretching exercises in chapter seven require focused attention and will help to raise your awareness of your body. For additional sensory-awareness exercises refer to chapter five.

Even while reading this you can momentarily put your attention into your body and allow your awareness to produce change. Are you really comfortable or are there areas of tension, strain and imbalance? If you notice any discomfort, just watch it for a moment and your body will respond with an impulse to rearrange itself. Check that your breathing is free and even. Try this now: close your eyes, go inside and ask your body how it would like to be and breathe. You may notice your mind interfering with comments; just observe them and return your focus to your breathing. That's enough for now, we will be going into awareness in greater detail later on but you may be able to keep the awareness of your breathing with you as you read.

WHERE ARE WE GOING?

So far we have been looking at the brain, how it orchestrates the complexities of balancing the body, how the mind interferes and the principles behind achieving results. Let us begin the process of change by finding out where you are and where you want to go. To recap, there are three essential ingredients to achieving results:

- A CLEAR AND REALISTIC GOAL
- NON-JUDGEMENTAL AWARENESS
- TRUST

If you were in the desert and needed to get to an oasis, your most important step would be to establish your current position.

It's all very well knowing the exact location of the oasis and that you want to get there but if you don't know where you are *now* you will go round and round in circles and may only stumble across it by accident, if at all. This way of achieving results can be thirsty work.

Where you are now is just as important as where you want to go – if not more so. You may be dissatisfied with what you can do and judge your performance as more or less worthless.

Nonetheless it is where you are and all you have. Value it. So I encourage you to let go of all thoughts of what sort of a skier you should be or ought to be and answer the questions as factually and honestly as you can!

So, who and where are you? I can assume with some certainty that you are either a man or a woman who has some desire to improve his or her skill on skis. I don't need to know more than that to be able to help you. However, *you* need to know a great deal more so that you can help yourself. The process is very simple. **By identifying exactly what you want from your skiing and finding out precisely where you are now, you will automatically have begun your journey towards the desired result.**

Personal Profile

The following questionnaires will help you to identify areas that may need attention and bring into focus what you might want to achieve in the future.

1. When did you start skiing?...
2. Was it your decision or someone else's? ....
3. Was it an enjoyable experience? ....
4. Did you take instruction?...
5. Was the class going at your pace? ....
6. How many weeks have you skied in total? ....
7. Rate on a scale of 1 to 5 how confident you feel on the following slopes, assuming reasonable conditions (5 = very confident, 1 = not very confident).
   Green............Blue............Red............Black............
8. Can you link turns in the fall-line?...
   On which type of slope? – green/blue/red/black....................
9. Describe your skiing on a 'good' day ....
10. Describe your skiing on a 'bad' day...
11. How do you perceive your ability in general?............................
12. What internal interference do you recognize? ....
13. How does it manifest externally? ....
14. Have you ever hurt yourself while skiing?...................................
15. Does this effect your current performance?.................................

16. How? ....
17. What is your height?........................ Weight?.............................
18. Do you take regular exercise? ....
19. Type?............................Frequency? ....
20. Do you do any pre-ski preparation? ....
21. Do you ever ski on an artificial slope? ....
22. Do you stretch or practise yoga? ....
23. What sports do you practise?..
24. What other sports have you practised in the past? ....
25. Why do you ski?...

I always ask my clients this last question. Some of their replies may help you compile your list. Write your reasons down in your notebook too – for future reference.

> Learn to ski
> Keep partner/children company
> Get fitter/for the exercise
> For the fresh air
> For the exhilaration
> Share holiday with friends
> Have fun
> Meet people/make new friends
> Get a suntan
> Relax
> Confront fear
> Enjoy the mountains
> Impress friends
> Express myself
> For the *après ski*

GETTING WHAT YOU WANT

If you are reading this book, I assume you would like to learn more about the sport so that you can ski better than you do now and enjoy it more. In order to do that you need to clarify exactly what you want, check that it is realistic and then take specific steps towards getting it.

Commitment is the fuel that will power you towards your

target. *Your 100 per cent commitment to a realistic goal is the key to success.* If, when doing the following exercise, you find you are unable to be completely committed to your specified goal, then you might want to redefine the goal so that you can be. Sometimes a lack of commitment indicates that the goal is unrealistic – a sure recipe for not achieving what you want.

This does not mean you cannot have dreams that may seem unattainable right now. You might be able to commit yourself to a realistic, attainable, intermediate goal that points towards that ideal. You may be a beginner who dreams of eventually skiing the steep and deep. While it may not seem within reach at the moment, don't discard it as your ultimate goal or be disappointed after a couple of years if you haven't reached this summit. Recognize the intermediate targets you need to achieve en route. These specific short-term goals can be as satisfying as the long-term dream. In this way you don't close the door on the dream and yet you can gain satisfaction from your commitment to the achievable. If all your short-term goals are attainable and your intention to achieve them unshakable, then success is assured. Nothing breeds success like success. So start creating it! Remember the Chinese proverb: 'A journey of a thousand miles must begin with a single step.'

To help you to get in touch with what you want, whether it is realistic and your level of commitment, please answer the following questions.

1. What do you want to achieve in the sport of skiing?
2. Is that realistic? ....
3. If not, what would be? ....
4. Would you like to ski: faster ....
                                     slower ....
                                     moguls ....
                                     powder ....
                                     ice ....
                                     other ....
5. Would you like to be: more relaxed ....
                                     more confident ....
                                     more flowing ....
                                     more efficient ....
                                     more controlled ....
                                     other ....
6. Would you like to have: more fun ....
                                     more style ....

7. Do you want to achieve your goals for yourself or for someone else?...

8. Can you choose to do them for yourself? ....

9. Choose some short-term goals for your next skiing holiday...

10. Are these goals realistic?...

11. If not, what would be? ....

12. How committed are you to your short-term goals? Rate each one on a scale of 1 to 10 (with 10 denoting complete commitment)..

13. Against the short-term goals rate on a scale of 1 to 10 where you are now. Goal is denoted by 10. What do you need to do to move from where you are now to a 10? ....

14. To make your holiday complete, add all the non-skiing activities that you would like to enjoy. Be sure these are compatible with your skiing goals. If you have decided you need to get more mileage and plan to ski from dawn to dusk every day, rather than lying around in the sun all afternoon, it may not be wise to include seven nights in the disco!

You may have already identified something specific that you need to do in order to achieve your goals. Here are some ideas and a note of the sections of *Skiing from the Inside* which can help you:

> Technical understanding...........................chapter 3
> Improved physical fitness........................chapter 7
> Develop awareness...................chapters 5, 6 and 7
> Different equipment.....................chapters 3 and 4
> Mental training/relaxation.....chapters 4, 6 and 7
> Support from coach/friend......chapters 5 and 6

You have now clarified where you are and what you want and you are already on the road to achieving results. In the next chapter we'll look at what happens to a body in motion and what influences us in the mountain environment.

Chapter Three

Balancing and the body

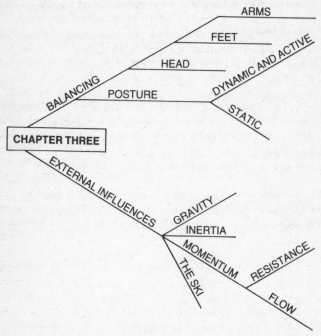

Having looked at some of the internal aspects of learning, it is now time to examine some of the external aspects of the sport – the physics and mechanics of skiing. There are literally dozens of books about ski technique; my aim in this chapter is to de-mystify the excessively analytical and mechanistic approach from which ski teaching suffers.

Wherever you ski, you will either have people giving you advice, whether they are qualified or not, or you will be watching other skiers and maybe copying what they are doing. It is useful to have some understanding of the fundamentals of effective movement on skis so that you can sort the wheat from the chaff and the truth from the illusion. If you can *feel* the movements that you make and evaluate what works and what doesn't, you will be able to direct your attention towards efficiency and effortlessness.

At the end of this chapter there are some exercises that you can do to help you improve your balance at home before you go skiing as well as out on the slopes. First let's have a look at some of the factors that influence our ability to balance on skis: the body, the design of the equipment and the effects of being in motion.

BEING LEVEL HEADED

It is hard to dissect the subject of how the body balances without making a nonsense, since every aspect is interconnected and the mechanism only works as a whole. Still, we need to be aware that imbalance in any part will upset the dynamics of the entire structure. The effects of inappropriate posture, holding back, insensitive feet and ankles, misusing the arms, misplacing the centre of mass or not anticipating inevitable changes in velocity can all contribute to good head plant technique. If the intellect can understand some of the facets of balancing and recognize certain laws of motion, then it can identify potential problems and begin to trust the body to do what it knows best.

The hidden conductor of the orchestra of muscle movements which create balance is in that head that we plant so frequently. A nerve in the ear sends signals from the cochlea to the brain to tell mission control whether the body is upright or falling and the brain responds with signals for recovery. *Balancing upright is only a series of linked recoveries and not a static position.*

The other senses – visual, auditory, tactile and proprioceptive – all provide essential input regarding our current and anticipated future whereabouts for processing. Anyone who has skied in a whiteout (flat light) will recall the feeling of loss of balance when only one of those senses is deprived of information.

In order to balance actively while in motion the eyes also need to be level. Some skiers bob their heads from side to side and give untold additional work to the information processing department. The head needs to be free to balance itself like a nautical compass on gimballs, allowing the eyes to stay level while the body flows underneath. That expression 'being level headed' has, perhaps, more layers of meaning than we realize.

THE POINT OF CONTACT

How well do you know your feet? If you are one of those who, with glazed look and wrinkled nose replies, 'Feet? Whose feet?,' prepare yourself. You may need a formal introduction to those protuberances at the end of your legs. In skiing their role is undervalued and their praises unsung. Surprising since they are the parts of the body that actually make contact with the ground. They are our connection, our point of balance.

Strong, sensitive feet are the hallmark of any athlete. If you can recognize the champions by their feet, the converse is also true. This is for many unfortunates where the rot starts, and I am not referring to athlete's foot. Sort the feet out and lots of other problems will take care of themselves. Expert skiers develop extremely sensitive feet which are a conduit for a mass of information relating to snow surface and feeling for fine ski-edge control, yet they must be athletic enough to create movement and resist the forces in a ski turn at speed. Educating the feet and allowing the brain constant feedback from the ever changing snow surface is essential if you want to ski skilfully. Experience on skis will condition your feet to respond automatically to the various demands made upon them but by becoming more aware of your feet before you go skiing you will speed up this process.

So, back to basics. Have a look at your feet. Are they long and wiry, short and wide, arched or flat? Do they tend to turn inwards or outwards when you walk? Can you wiggle your toes? Can you separate your toes like a fan? Point your toes like a ballerina? Curl them up? Can you get them to work for you? Can you walk on the balls of your feet as if on high heels? Can you spring off your toes, land silently like a fairy and spring again into the air?

If you have discovered that your feet are like aliens, start to raise your awareness of them right away. At the end of this chapter you will find some awareness and balancing exercises. The exercises in chapter seven will also help bring life to your feet and subsequently greater sensitivity to your skiing.

GRAVITY – SERIOUS STUFF

Hopefully you are participating with more than just your intellect and actually made the effort to explore your feet just now. When you were finding out if you could spring off the ground, did you think about what brings you back to earth with such regularity? In skiing this happens more often than we would perhaps like.

Sir Isaac Newton observed that objects attract each other and proposed a force he called gravity, which is directly proportional to the product of their masses. If there was no such thing as gravitational pull, you would have flown off like a fairy just now, balance would be an irrelevance and we would have no need for ski lifts. Gravity keeps us and apple trees planted on the planet: the mass of the earth has an irresistible attraction to both.

The effect of gravity would have us lying around like beached whales were it not for the design of the human organism, which enables us to balance upright and use our limbs for propulsion. Rather like the air we breathe, which we take for granted until it is polluted or denied us, gravity is always with us – whether we are conscious of it or not. Skiing is one sport that brings it smartly to our attention. Skiers are always at the mercy of gravity: it is gravity that powers us down a slope and gravity that takes over when we lose balance. Gravity is at the heart of skiing: it is what attracts us to this game of sliding and yet for many of us it is what we are most afraid of. Learning how to flow with it rather than resist it is the ultimate sensation. Playing with gravity is the art of skiing and this game is just as available to a beginner as an expert.

So, what are the forces that are generated as a result of being propelled by gravity and how do our bodies cope? First let's have a look at how the body deals with stationary balancing. That is, when we are standing upright but not going anywhere.

BALANCING – STATIC MODE

When we are standing, the weight of the body is on the heels and the body mass is directly over the feet. The arms can hang relaxed by the sides or in a variety of positions. The head may be tilted to the side and the eyes unfocused. The attitude of the body can be passive and there doesn't seem to be a lot going on but all the while the muscles of the feet, legs and trunk are quietly keeping the skeleton erect. Very clever stuff.

We can walk using this 'static' posture, with our weight on our heels, but if we want to move quickly, then our bodies must use an entirely different posture. To travel faster we need to produce more power from our legs and to withstand the additional forces caused by this extra motion. This change in posture between walking and running usually happens automatically but some people have developed poor posture and need assistance to return to a more effective shape. Many skiers have postural problems as a result of poor teaching or from asymmetrical patterns of movement learned whilst anxious or afraid. The exercises in chapter seven will help you to develop a balanced structure.

BALANCING – DYNAMIC MODE

To flow with gravity and cope with the external forces generated by this motion over a slippery, tilted surface our bodies have to change shape. The body's natural reaction to the first indication of sliding is to resist by leaning back and digging in the heels. *It is crucial for beginners to spend time sliding and learning to become calm, loose and balanced over the skis as the sliding continues.* Orientation in this radically different world requires body awareness, active vision, alert hearing, and dynamic, active balancing. Like a tennis player at the net, we need to adopt a posture or body shape that is ready for forward motion, and prepared for everchanging terrain and snow conditions.

For the skier, dynamic active balancing differs from static balancing in several ways:

**   The centre of gravity lowers by flexing hips, knees and ankles.

**   The weight moves forwards and is distributed over the whole foot with the instep and ball of the foot most actively used.

**   When turning, the centre of mass does not stay over the feet, but inclines inwards.

** The pelvis tilts upwards slightly so that the legs can become active.

** The arms move forwards and outwards, hanging freely from the shoulders, ready to assist in balancing, with the backs of the hands facing slightly forwards.

** The head remains still with the eyes level and actively reading the terrain.

** The legs are prepared to open sideways quickly to provide a wider base of support.

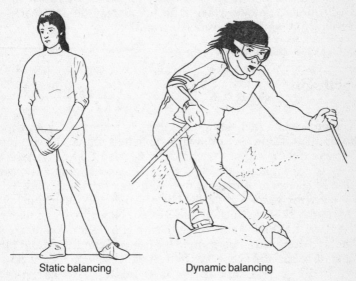

Static balancing   Dynamic balancing

Fig. 3.1

In Fig. 3.1 you can see the differences between static and active balancing: two very different ways of keeping upright. Many skiers start off in a static balancing mode and wonder why they bite the dust. They may adopt that approach because in skiing the legs aren't obviously moving, as in walking or running. Skiing appears to be 'static', a game of standing on two sliding planks. In fact this is not the case at all. On skis it is particularly important to lower the centre of mass and adopt a slightly crouched posture in order not to be thrown onto the heels as the skis begin to slide, leaving the body behind. Even though it may not appear to be necessary, it is wise to get into the habit of assuming a 'ready for anything' dynamic position before we start moving.

Visualise a tennis player about to make a winning return or put a volley away. Why do you think she does all those little bounces from the ball of one foot to the other? She is alert and ready for anything – active and dynamic. To make it real for you, stand up, be still for a few moments then assume an active stance. Notice how you experience the transition from static to dynamic balancing. Although you can adopt the posture for dynamic balancing when static, it is virtually impossible to run with your body in static mode. Have a go – you may be amused by the result. No wonder it doesn't work on skis!

THE SKI

Understanding that skis are designed to respond to your actions, to do the turning for you, will establish trust that the equipment is there to help rather than hinder you. Many skiers imagine that skis are just planks which have to be heaved about and waste untold energy in lifting and throwing their bodies around.

Over the years a great deal of research and development has gone into ski construction and design. Nowadays, the materials combine lightness with strength and durability. There are skis that are designed to perform in a variety of conditions and others that have specific properties to deal with the extremes of powder snow or ice and differences in an individual's strength and weight.

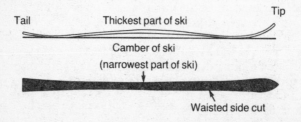

Fig. 3.2 The Skiing Machine

Whatever type they are, all skis have common characteristics which are worth noting (Fig. 3.2). Like an arrow, the ski has a pointed tip and a blunt tail. When you lie the ski on the ground, there is an inbuilt camber so that when you add your weight it lies flat on the snow. When a ski is flat on the snow, it will glide in a straight line.

The ski is wider at the tip and tail and narrower at the waist. This sidecut has some influence on the radius of the turn that the ski will favour.

When put on edge and pressure is applied, it flexes into reverse camber and will turn in a curved arc. It is the shape of this reverse camber which will most influence the radius of the turn. Realizing that skis are gliding *and* turning machines may alter the way you ride and guide them. I have met countless skiers who were astounded to hear that the ski is actually designed to turn them and that, once on edge and pressured into reverse camber, it will inscribe an arc in the snow. With additional rotation of the legs and feet precise steering is possible. Trusting that the ski is designed to turn can transform your relationship with your equipment and increase confidence overnight.

THE FORCES AT PLAY

Like riding a bicycle, balancing on skis actually becomes easier once you get moving. One of the beauties of being in motion is that we can play with gravity, the force that pulls us down the mountain, and use the forces that result from turning to keep us from falling. This dance with the mountain is the essence of skiing for me. It can be both an uplifting and a humbling experience, for the mountain is constant: a standard against which to measure our ability to respond to its contours, changing snow conditions and the laws of motion.

If you are a beginner, you may find that you cannot fully make sense of the following because you have few experiences to which you can refer. Please do not worry, knowing all about the laws of motion will not necessarily help you to ski. Not being a scientist myself, I hope my style is simple enough to follow, but, if some of the explanations seem too complicated, skip them and just read the parts that you can understand.

If we skiers could travel at the speed of light, perhaps we would not turn to Isaac Newton for answers. Fortunately, in attempting an understanding of the forces at play in skiing, Newton provides us with some simpler explanations than Albert Einstein. Understanding these laws may not change our ability to control a pair of skis, but when face down in the snow, the recognition that a movable force had just met an immovable object might be a consolation.

Newton's First Law states that *a body remains at rest or in uniform motion in a straight line unless acted upon by an external, unbalanced force.* To get your body mass moving you need muscles or gravity to counteract this tendency, which is known as 'inertia'. Inertia is what must be overcome before any action is underway. Getting out of bed in the morning is a great example. It takes a bit of effort to get going but once we break through the inertia we are up and away and inertia then contributes to our momentum.

Once in motion down a slope and under the effects of gravity and momentum some resistance (i.e. an 'external force' as in Newton's First Law) must be created in order to deflect momentum to alter direction and/or control speed. In skiing it is not always desirable to take every slope straight from top to bottom. By turning and lengthening the route we can avoid obstacles or control our speed.

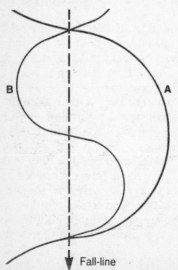

B   A

Fig. 3.3
A = long radius turn
B = two shorter radius turns

Fall-line

GRAVITY – FRIEND OR FOE?

Surrendering, even momentarily, to the terminal velocity of a given slope is the secret of skiing. Far too much emphasis is placed on resisting gravity rather than flowing with it. Somehow our minds get set into a defensive pattern of behaviour and gravity becomes the 'bad guy'. For whatever reason, most skiers spend their time avoiding the pull of gravity and from this defensive stance are unable to cope when it grabs them. They then resist even more by going onto their heels and taking all sorts of avoiding action. The result – gravity 1 skier 0.

To ski skilfully gravity must become our friend, not our enemy. In this partnership we must surrender to its power and influence and then, and only then, can we truly choose how much latitude we allow it. One of the many paradoxes in skiing is that we only gain control of gravity when we give up trying to control it.

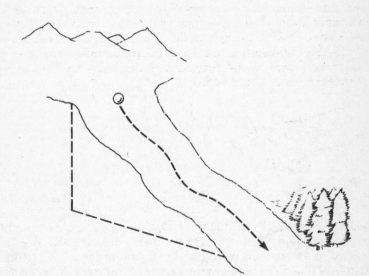

Fig. 3.4 A slope showing the fall-line, the line of least resistance a ball would take.

So, when starting to ski, learning to flow down a gentle slope with a flat run-out or counter-slope so that you can maintain balance both physically and emotionally is essential. The greater the tilt, the easier it is for gravity to pull you towards the centre of the earth. So make sure that the slope is shallow enough for you to surrender willingly to the power of gravity. At this stage anxiety can unsettle dynamic balancing. It is important to go with the flow, to enjoy the sensation of gravity pulling you downwards. As you feel this directional pull down the line of least resistance, the fall-line (Fig. 3.4) you will notice that acceleration ceases as you reach terminal velocity. This will differ according to the tilt and length of the slope, the friction of your skis and amount of air resistance.

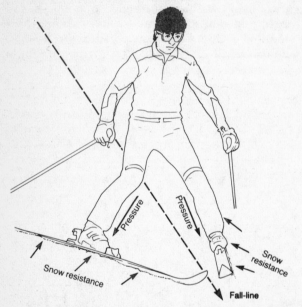

Fig. 3.5

The snowplough is usually the first form of resistance taught on gentle terrain, where it can slow down a descent. Both skis are pushed at an angle to the flow of momentum (Fig. 3.5) and the degree of plough determines the degree of control. It is, however, not the complete answer to control since all it produces is a skidded, braking effect, in which some momentum is lost through resistance due to snow displacement.

Nevertheless, ploughing is a useful means of discovering how to steer your skis and of learning the fundamentals of turning the legs, edging and pressuring. All these skills can be refined into more controlled 'carving' turns later on. When you are ploughing without creating very much resistance, if one ski has less pressure applied to it than the other, the resistance is no longer equal and a deflection to one side will result. If the body is balancing dynamically, the skier does not have to make any additional movement for the skis to make a skidded deflection. By learning to commit more and more body weight and to pressurize the turning, outside ski, greater control and response will be experienced.

Rotation of the hips to the outside of the turn or over rotation of the shoulders at the end of the turn are the most common problems that beginner and intermediate skiers encounter. Indeed, hip rotation is probably the most common inhibiting factor to progress, and many intermediates remain on a learning plateau until this is resolved. The excessive movement of the upper body disturbs stability and tends to flatten the skis, resulting in a loss of control. Hip rotation develops as a result of poor instruction, brute force and ignorance of how a ski turns.

The snowplough, in which the centre of mass is placed automatically inside both skis, is the basis of the more complex parallel turn. But you rush your progress at your peril. Like a rose, if you force the bud to open before it is time, you will end up with a deformed flower.

THE PARALLEL MYTH

For years, ski schools have been pushing parallel turns, and skiers are conditioned to think that getting the feet together is the means to the end. The 'when my skis are together I will have solved everything' dream. True, parallel turns look smooth, stylish and cool. They symbolize control of the monster gravity. The problem is that everyone is in such a rush to get parallel that real mastery is sacrificed for short-term gain. The cart is put before the proverbial horse. In fact, true parallel skiing is the result of having signed an alliance between your momentum, the outside, turning ski and the snow. *Parallel is the effect not the cause.*

Fortunately, many ski teachers now recognize the feet-together syndrome for the myth it is. Sadly, what most skiers interpret as feet jammed together is anything but. When a line of soldiers does a right wheel, the guy on the outside is doing a great deal more than the chap on the inside. Nevertheless they seem to be a single unit. It is the same with skiing parallel. By adopting a narrow 'racing snowplough' at higher speeds or even simply a wider stance, and discovering greater commitment to balancing against the outside ski while turning, you will solve the riddle of what looks like skiing with the 'feet together'. The key here is independent leg action and trusting the ski to turn.

So, with Newton's First Law in mind, the force that causes a ski to turn is snow resistance. Resistance is set up between the snow and the ski. It is a centripetal force, i.e. the snow resistance causes movement towards a centre (Fig. 3.6). The precise nature of the force is the result of ski design, construction, maintenance and use.

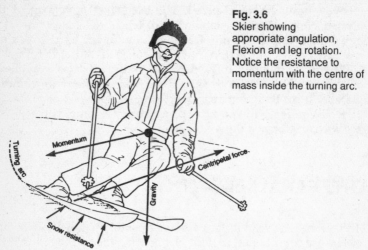

Fig. 3.6
Skier showing
appropriate angulation,
Flexion and leg rotation.
Notice the resistance to
momentum with the centre of
mass inside the turning arc.

Without getting too technical, once in motion if a ski is under pressure, on its edge and turned at an angle to the direction of travel the result is a turning arc. This arc usually involves some drift or skidding, a result of momentum wanting the body mass to carry on in the original direction of travel. Imagine you are driving a car round a corner at speed. It will tend to tilt towards the outside of the curve and perhaps even lose traction and slide to the outside if the road is wet or icy.

When steering your skis in a turn, it is the resulting changes of shape, both to the snow and to your body, which are significant. The snow is displaced to make an indented track while the body compensates for the pull of momentum to the outside of the turn by maintaining the centre of mass inside the turning arc. In a snowplough this happens automatically. The ski is on edge, turned across the direction of travel, and there is an inward inclination of both legs and the resulting pressure when in motion can be felt through the foot. The upper body is flexed forwards at the hips to counteract the effect of speed, and, in order not to topple over by banking the whole body inwards, it remains facing the direction of momentum while the thighs rotate in the pelvis to steer the skis, directing the path of the turn. This gives rise to the curved shape of a skier, called 'angulation', which is sometimes misinterpreted as a sideways bending of the waist.

You can begin to explore this right now. Stand up, get into your dynamic balancing mode and, while facing forwards, turn your feet to the side. If you do this on a slippery floor, you can slide your feet from side to side. Can you see your thighs wanting to travel in the same direction as your feet? Your legs are actually rotating in your hip joints underneath your still upper body. If you stand tall and try the same foot turning, you will notice how limited your range of movement is in this undynamic posture.

FLOWING FROM CENTRE

Your centre of mass is the focal point for all the forces of balance. Your arms may flail and you may lean like the Tower of Pisa but you will hit the deck only if your mass moves beyond an untenable position in relation to your point of contact with the planet.

When the body is upright, muscles work like guy ropes to keep the skeleton centred over the feet. When the alignment of the skeleton and the oscillation of muscles are at optimum – i.e. maximum efficiency for least effort – perfect structural balance has been achieved. To maintain this, while in motion on skis, additional muscular activity is required to keep the body mass stable in relation to constantly changing forces.

When a person first starts to ski he or she usually exhibits a high level of tension and puts more effort than necessary into each movement. There is also little awareness of the centre of mass. As confidence and a feel for the actions develop, the awkwardness disappears. More efficiency and a greater sense of balance are experienced.

As a skier first begins to slide on skis and steer while ploughing something very exciting happens – a sudden awareness of being a body in 'motion'.

Words cannot describe what it is to connect with an energy that is neither self-generated nor motorized and to feel able to manipulate its effect on your body. This is a crucial moment in learning to ski when emotions, creating excessive tension and resistance, can, if you are not careful, interfere with good balancing. Inappropriate patterns of movement can become habitual and plague progress at every subsequent level.

BALANCING RESISTANCE AND FLOW

As a competitive mogul skier I became very aware of a connection with the flow. Forced to confront the fall-line and to minimize my emotional response I would use the image of water taking the line of least resistance down through the moguls. Of flowing.

The secret of skilful skiing lies in the smoothness of the skier's flow down the slope and from one turn to the next. Newton's Second Law has significance here. He stated that *the rate of change of momentum is proportional to the force causing it, and occurs in the direction of that force.* If your mind boggles on that one, don't worry. It simply means that if you want to turn quickly and at speed you need big forces applied quickly. If you want to turn less or on long arcs, then lesser forces are required over longer periods of time. It also means that you need to become aware of the direction of your total momentum at all times.

Since our bodies are jointed and hopefully not rigid while skiing, our different body parts have their own momentum and our sensitivity to both our centre of mass and how the placement of our limbs affects that mass will determine how dynamic and flowing our skiing is. A skater spinning fast with arms wrapped closely into the body will hold the arms out wide to increase the moment of inertia and thereby slow down the speed of the rotation. In skiing we can often stabilize our upper bodies by holding our arms out further.

Every ski turn is made in relation to the tilt of the slope and a chosen speed. The essence of skiing is finding the balance between creating resistance and encouraging or allowing flow. Every ski turn has an element of both, and the 'perfect' turn is the one in which there is optimum flow and appropriate resistance. Just as a conker flies off at a tangent if the string breaks, so a skier tends to be pulled at a tangent to the arc of a turn. The skier's flow is thus not directly down the fall-line. In order to steer a new turn the skier resists their own flow by edging the skis and turning them at an angle to the flow of the previous arc. This build-up of resistance deflects the flow downhill where gravity adds more energy.

SKIING FROM CENTRE

When I ski, I feel there is a special relationship between my centre of mass and its flow line, the pull of gravity and my feet. This virtually hidden aspect of maintaining perfect balance comes from an awareness of my relationship with resistance and flow. When turning down a slope, the most efficient, effective skiers keep their centres moving close to the fall-line while their skis stay in contact with the snow and take a much longer route. This illusion of stillness at the centre of the body hides a fair amount of activity as muscles in the feet, legs, buttocks, lower back and stomach work to maintain dynamic posture, active balancing and steering.

In Fig.3.7 you will see the different routes that the feet, centre of mass and head take down a slope. In this fluid relationship the 'centre' and feet move to best serve each other with the upper body balancing quietly on top. Either the centre is placed so that the skis can be driven or the feet are moved to balance the centre most effectively.

You may be wondering where your centre is. Your centre of mass can be found somewhere around your navel. It is not a fixed spot and will be lower with boots and skis on. If you pay attention to the area below your navel, you will be close. Do the centring exercises at the end of this chapter to discover more about it. What you are after is a sense of the centre of gravitational pull – a directional heaviness. In certain extreme bending postures your centre of mass may actually be outside your body, however the sensation will still be experienced within.

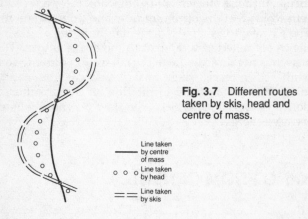

Fig. 3.7 Different routes taken by skis, head and centre of mass.

——— Line taken by centre of mass

o o o Line taken by head

= = Line taken by skis

By 'skiing from centre' you can become aware of changes in terrain and the balance of those opposites, resistance and flow. It is easy to become obsessed with the individual movements that the parts of the body are making, and to see each ski turn as separate from all others. Remember to spend time getting in touch with the feel of total motion, the feel of the path of your centre in relation to the general fall-line of the slope, i.e. *your* flow-line in relation to the general fall-line of the hillside. With this central focus, your brain can best orchestrate the whole dance and harmonize with what is often an unpredictable partner – the snow-covered mountain.

MAINTAINING EQUILIBRIUM

Newton's Third Law states that *for every action there is an equal and opposite reaction.* This has many implications for you as a skier.

Any movement of any part of your body requires an opposite movement or reaction to compensate and maintain stability. Movements of the legs have to be counterbalanced with a movement of the upper body and vice versa. On the other hand, when you lose balance, an appropriate 're-action' of the arms can re-establish equilibrium. Observe yourself in a simple activity like walking or running; as one leg moves forward, the opposite arm automatically compensates for the disturbance. In skiing it is particularly important that we anticipate changes in terrain and the effects of the movements we make.

The day a friend drew my attention to my arms and hands my skiing made one of those yearned for quantum leaps. 'Imagine you are holding a tray of drinks. You are only earning tips so you mustn't spill a drop.' Sure, the martinis sloshed about and the beer slopped all over the tray but my windmill arms were reasonably still for the first time. Instead of getting left behind on every turn and not being ready for the next one, my hands were just where I needed them. (If you do this exercise with your ski poles as the tray, hold them out in front of you with the backs of the hands uppermost to encourage effective posture.)

Now this is one of those chicken and egg situations. Arms are both balancers and unbalancers. It depends on what you do with them and when. We don't realize just how much we depend on them to help us balance in our automatic everyday activities: walking, standing, sitting down and standing up. In skiing they are crucial stabilizers. The backwards-rowing, banana-skin response is the classic last-ditch effort by the body to remain vertical before the horizontal body slam.

Strange that such clever appendages become so distorted on the slopes where they are either over used, under used or just plain abused. Many inexperienced instructors tend to demonstrate with stiff, posed, awkward arms – as if their jackets still had the hangers in them. Even more bizarre is the would-be racer who, on an open slope, knocks non-existent poles out of the way with aggressive, useless flourishes. Both are aesthetically displeasing as well as a waste of effort; the latter, in particular, causes undesirable reactions in the legs which in turn upset the skis. Arms, after all, connect to shoulders and affect the whole of the body. Remember Sir Isaac's words *for every action there is an equal and opposite reaction*.

When I asked 'extreme' skier Glen Plake what he is most aware of in his body while skiing down the world's steepest

slopes, he replied, 'My hands. If they aren't OK, then nothing else
is.'

Arms and hands mirror the effects of what we are doing
elsewhere. I view mine as tension meters. If I find I'm gripping
my poles, I know that there's some anxiety, and consequently
some imbalance, lurking around. If this is allowed to develop, the
next stage is dragging the pole in the snow to slow myself down
– not very effective but a comfort!

Ideally, your arms need to be loose and yet alert and your
hands visible within lower peripheral vision and ready to plant
the pole to trigger a new turn with as little disturbance as
possible to the rest of the body. If the general posture is dynamic,
then the arms can hang 'forwards' from the shoulders (because
the body is tilted) and, if allowed to, they will naturally move
outwards to balance.

'Where do I put the pole?' is one of the standard questions
beginners ask. There is no set place in the snow in relation to
your skis but only an appropriate place in relation to your
momentum and towards the centre of your new turn.

As beginners, dealing with an abnormal slippery world, the
ski poles may be viewed as the only remaining props. Another
pair of legs, as it were. Hopefully this phase soon passes, and
although a seemingly brutal exercise, skiing without poles at the
beginning can help a skier develop better balance.

Some people hold their poles very high, which is exhausting,
and others keep them pinned to their sides, tensed with fear.
Others are like windmills with a variety of wild, flailing
movements. In essence the arms have to move very little, with
only the wrist making a semi-circular motion and cocking action
to move the pole from the carrying position to the plant position.
After the pole plant, as the body moves past, the pole
automatically goes back to carrying position so there's usually no
need to hoick it out.

There is no one way to do it. Light touches may work in some
conditions and not in others. A heavy-handed, strong-arm
technique can provide a momentary widening of support to
assist balance at the start of a turn on a steep slope or in moguls.
To counteract the reaction of the upper body to a very fast
rotation of the legs the pole can be planted very firmly. This
requires a strong upper body to withstand the increase in inertia
temporarily borrowed from the earth, and the trick is to get the
pole to come with you when the moment is passed.

The secret of effective arms, hands and pole planting lies in raising your awareness of what they are doing, letting go of inappropriate tension and allowing them to be as 'natural' as possible. There is no 'set' position, no 'pose'. They must be allowed to respond to the demands of dynamic balance and harmonize with the whole body in motion.

BALANCING EXERCISES

Increasing your awareness

** Take a few minutes to feel the movements you can make with your feet. Stand in bare feet, with the feet hip width apart and the *outsides* of the feet parallel. That may mean that you feel slightly pigeon toed.

** Elongate the toes as much as possible. Feel the three main points of contact: the heel, the joint of the big toe and the joint of the little toe. Notice the differences between the two feet. Rock gently forwards and backwards, moving from toes to heels and back again.

** Notice the main arch which spans from the ball of the foot to the heel and lift your inner ankle-bone slightly, keeping the big toe joint firmly down. Move the knees from side to side without dropping the inner arch. Feel the edges of your feet.

** The next stage is to put on your ski boots and retain this level of awareness. Let your feet remain alive and responsive inside your boots. Movement will be limited by the form of the boot but you should still be able to jump into the air off your toes, land quietly and jump from foot to foot, pressing strongly against the instep.

The way we stand on our feet influences how we walk, run, move and ski. By increasing your awareness of your feet, you may uncover problems that need resolving through exercise or correction (see chapter seven). The effort required to do this will seem small when you reap the rewards of greater athleticism and ability to balance.

Improving your balance

** Stand on one leg with a slightly bent knee for a couple of moments. Let your foot and arms make all the necessary corrections to your balance. Change legs. Do extra time on the weaker leg. You could do this daily as you brush your teeth. Notice how your foot and leg compensate as you move your head and the toothbrush.

** Stand stiffly with your back to a friend. Imagine you are a sentry, static and unmoving. Ask your friend to push you gently either forwards or from side to side. Notice how easily you topple off balance, like a lead soldier. Now choose an image that conveys something firmly rooted but whose structure blends and flows with any force: a willow in the wind, for example. See the image clearly in your mind and let your partner push you again. Allow your body to go with the wind as it is pushed and flow back to centre.

Improving balance on skis

Once you are on skis, you can help yourself balance with the awareness exercises in chapter five and the following exercises and games.

** On a flat surface choose an object to walk towards. Now walk towards another target without using your poles. Change your style of walking: walk tall like a giant and then walk small like a little creature. Now walk fast with little steps and slow with a longer stride. Do this with and without your poles.

** Remember roller or ice skating? Skate on your skis and let yourself glide, keeping your body mass over the gliding ski.

** Now have a race with a friend, choosing different ways of getting to your finishing post - skating, walking or sliding.

** Once you are sliding down a slope with confidence, see if you can balance on one leg.

Moving from centre

** Get up and walk purposefully towards an object. Notice if you lead with your head or with your centre. Most people tend to poke their heads forward whereas a ballerina or gymnast, who has a highly developed sense of balance, will automatically walk 'from centre'. Now walk forwards 'from centre' and notice the difference.

** With your awareness in your centre, practise raising and lowering that point while staying balanced over the whole of both feet. You may have to place your feet slightly apart to maintain balance. This raising and lowering may bring new meaning to the traditional and much misunderstood exhortation 'bend ze knees'.

** Stand with your feet wider apart, lower your centre and do some hip rotations with your eyes closed. Pretend you are a belly dancer. Tip your pelvis down and up. From a mid position, inscribe imaginary figures of eight, using your navel to outline the shape on a horizontal plane from side to side and fore and aft.

You may find you have a hollow back, are very stiff in your hips or are unable to tip your pelvis up and down. It is well worth doing something about this to avoid lower-back problems and to improve your edge control and balance on skis. Please refer to the stretching exercises in chapter seven.

** Do some jumps from side to side, lifting your centre over the support foot. Then add some forward propulsion and make a zig-zag path. Let your centre lead the movement rather than your feet. Feel your centre moving from side to side.

** When you next go skiing, pay attention to your centre and notice where your navel is pointing in relation to the fall-line of the slope. If you find that it points across or up the hill at the end of a turn, it may indicate that you are rotating your hips excessively.

** Become more familiar with your centre by noticing where it is in relation to the arc of the outside ski in each turn. Ideally, it should be inside the arc and flowing across your skis and into the new turn. You may find your legs keep resisting the pull to the outside of the turn. Let your mass flow across into the new turn a little earlier.

** Your navel needs to be 'open' to your flow line. Imagine that there is a light shining out of your navel: it will help you to become more aware of what is going on. Let the light shine in the direction that your mass is flowing down the slope. Check that your lower back is not hollow by shining the light straight ahead, and not up in the air or down at the ground.

If you have been able to follow the more technical aspects of the last two chapters, hopefully you will begin to relate them to your experience rather than keeping them as purely intellectual input. They are intended as a framework for your expanding awareness of what is actually happening. If you found Newton's Laws hard to grasp, don't worry about them. Either way, when in action *feeling* what is happening is more relevant than trying to figure out the laws of motion. The next two chapters will help you to do just that.

Chapter Four

Setting the scene for learning

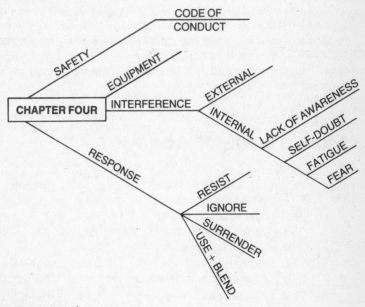

SAFETY

To self-coach you'll need to adopt habits that will support the process and take responsibility for both your internal and external experience. When starting to ski, being in the mountains may be overwhelming initially so it is always a good idea to be with others in a place specifically designated for beginners. In some European countries we are fortunate to have dry ski slopes where we can practise skiing all year and where beginners can cover the basics, saving a great deal of time and trouble before arriving out on the snow. Once in the mountains, you may wish to be in the care of a ski school who will take some of the initial responsibility for your welfare and guide your progress. It is crucial that you are not overstressed so don't follow your more experienced friends to the top of the mountain yet!

Those who have skied before will need a piste map or a local expert to help them find their way around a new resort. Like the sea, the mountain has its own rules. Keeping yourself in one piece is part of becoming a skilful skier. Minimizing the risk of injury, to yourself and to others is a priority. The growing popularity of the sport means that skiing sometimes resembles motorway driving with occasional rush-hour bottlenecks. Familiarize yourself with the internationally recognized Skiers' Code of Conduct. It is based on common-sense principles and in some ski resorts (particularly in the USA) this 'highway code' is being enforced with penalties.

SKIER'S CODE OF CONDUCT

1. A skier's conduct should in no way prejudice or endanger others.
2. A skier must ski in control at all times. Be able to stop when necessary and avoid other skiers.
3. Slower skiers have right of way.
4. The overtaking skier must give wide margin to the overtaken skier and not impede the slower skier's path.
5. A skier must avoid stopping, whenever possible, in the middle of a piste or narrow trail. Move to the side, as soon as possible, to ensure the safety and free passage of other skiers.
6. When it is necessary to walk or climb near a piste, use only the side of the trail; never walk or climb in the middle.
7. The skier entering the main slope from an intersecting piste must give way to skiers on the main slope.
8. Before starting off or when crossing another track, look first to make sure the way is clear.

9. Observe and obey all piste signs placed to control downhill skiing and the use of lifts. At all times cooperate with the representatives of the ski lift company and the ski patrol.

In addition, may I suggest the following safety tips:

1. Never ski alone.

2. Warm up before setting off down a slope.

3. Be aware of your energy level.

4. When stopping by another skier, if possible always stop below in case you lose control. This is particularly important on steep slopes.

5. In the case of an accident, protect the injured person by crossing skis vertically in the snow above the site as a warning to other skiers. Send two competent, cool-headed skiers from your party to alert the ski patrol with details of the nearest numbered piste marker or enrol the services of a passer-by.

6. Recognize that skiing 'off piste' is the domain of the qualified guide. A mountain guide, unlike a ski instructor or a tour operator's piste guide, is a member of the UIAGM (Union International des Associations des Guides de Montagne). Their rigorous training, intimate local knowledge and years of experience mean that only they can competently lead you. Many skiers make the mistake of thinking that their expertise is a passport to safety in the mountain wilderness. True, their legs may get them out there but will the mountain allow them a return ticket?

7. Don't jump the lift queue.

8. Keep to the tow track while going up a drag lift.

9. Get off only at the top of the lift – look out for the dismount warning signs.

10. Let go of the t-bar or poma carefully and move away quickly.

11. Carry your skis carefully – mind other people's heads!

12. Do not use freestyle or alpine-racing competition or training sites unless you have permission.

13. Do not ski along nordic/cross-country skiing trails with downhill equipment.

EQUIPMENT

HOT TIPS BELOW ZERO

We need to be aware of the potential harshness of the mountain environment, where temperatures can soar or plummet. Our clothing must cater for the extremes of sweating or freezing as well as often intense physical activity, and we have to develop a different sort of dress sense. Being over or under-dressed will affect our enjoyment and ultimately influence our survival.

The secret of remaining comfortable on the slopes is to keep warm and dry. In Europe temperatures can range from -30ºC to +10ºC throughout the ski season and during each day the skier can experience anything from chilly, early-morning shade to blazing, high-altitude sun at noon.

Modern technology has provided us with the answer to the contradictory requirements of water and wind-resistant fabrics which can 'breathe'. To cope with extremes, we can use the latest lightweight insulation and the principle of trapping air between several layers of clothing without resorting to massive weight or bulk. With attention paid to effective closure at ankles, wrists, waist and neck; and a hood, ski clothing nowadays can be both fashionable and functional, a far cry from the tweeds of the post-war pioneers.

Good quality leather gloves or mitts are an essential investment, particularly for a beginner who is likely to come into contact with the snow more frequently. Remaining warm and dry is again the key to comfort, so buy the best and they will last for years. Quality thermal underwear (a long-sleeved vest and long johns) will also make a huge difference. Although a cotton or silk feel best against the skin, man-made fibres, designed to wick perspiration away from the body, dry more quickly once wet. If long johns are figure-hugging they will help to raise body awareness by giving you more precise feedback of limb movement.

When skiing the knee joints need to be able to move freely. I find that additional warmers, made from neoprene or wool, keep my knees ready for action even in the coldest weather. The sleeve of an old sweater can be sewn over your long underwear to create extra warmth where it is needed. If you buy neoprene warmers, make sure that there is no pressure over the knee cap and that they do not restrict circulation.

FROM SUN TO SNOW

As lowlanders, learning about wind, snow and the intensity of high-altitude sun can be a painful process. Special sunglasses and facial skin-cream are essential protection against harmful ultraviolet rays. Weather conditions can be deceiving: wind-blown snow can hinder your vision just as much as a snowstorm so it is always wise to have goggles with you. A small backpack containing a warm scarf, hat, goggles, sun screen, extra gloves, some high-energy food and enough space for an extra layer of clothing will ensure your comfort in all weather conditions.

SKI BINDINGS

Bindings are a bit like seat belts; there are times when you want them to keep you firmly in place and times when you want to exit pronto. Binding manufacturers don't guarantee their products will release so keep them maintained. Get an expert to check and lubricate the release mechanism and control the release settings regularly. The anti-friction pads that facilitate the binding release when pressure builds against the boot can go missing or become rough and worn so replace them when necessary. Ice and snow packed under the boot can also alter performance. Grit and dirt in the mechanism will inhibit proper functioning so protect bindings when travelling.

BOOTS

The ski boot is the other vital connection between you and the ski. They need to fit snugly and suit your level of expertise. For beginners and intermediates the most crucial factor is being able to flex forwards easily at the ankle. If a boot is too rigid and blocks ankle flexion and extension, the body will be unable to adopt the appropriate posture. The telltale signs are either a lowering of the posterior, accompanied by a feeling of 'being in the back seat', or a forward jackknifing of the upper body to absorb uneven terrain, like a hen pecking corn. Either way the body mass is in a state of potential imbalance.

Sore feet can ruin your enjoyment and badly fitting boots can interfere with your ability to respond appropriately. Being a bit of a princess, I'm on my knees at the first sign of a pressure point and consider comfortable feet a priority. If you decide to buy boots and want to ensure comfort and a good fit, make friends with your local ski-shop boot fitter or find out some of the tricks of the trade. You can begin by disposing of a couple of myths.

Firstly, some people actually do not realize that accurate fit and comfort can make good bedfellows. As Cinderella will tell you, correct sizing is fundamental. Toes must have enough room to move and stay warm while the rest of the foot needs to feel good and snug. After that the shell of the boot can be 'pushed out' in places where there is excessive pressure from bunions. To relieve pressure from bony ankles or lumps on heels, add extra padding, or high-density foam doughnuts. Even taking a knife to the inner boot can turn Cinders into a princess at a well-planned stroke.

Grandad's thick, ribbed socks are no longer *de rigueur*. Finer, thinner socks provide a more comfortable answer provided they remain wrinkle-free. Jamming your long johns or snow cuffs down the front of the boot will form a ridge on your shin just where you need smooth contact. Remove friction from a sore spot either by padding with sponge or by placing two thin layers of plastic bag between the sock and the tongue of the inner boot – sweaty but smooth. Whichever ruse you choose, make sure you have two smooth surfaces and can press your shins forwards firmly and comfortably against the tongue.

The second myth is that ski boots have to be done up very tight. This is perhaps a hangover from the days of leather boots and laces. Nowadays, with plastic shells, boots only need to be fastened firmly around the ankle. The top buckle in the classic style of boot can be left loose and will assist in flexing forwards.

Many foot problems can be solved in an instant by loosening the tension.

For those with my problem, poor circulation, invest in one of the new range of heated boots. Hedonism rules just fine in my book and having warm feet is essential. In fact, heated boots have even deprived me of my old excuse for falling over my feet. However, cold feet may indicate more than just a circulatory deficiency. Often they stem from excessive tension associated more with temperament than temperature. Check whether you are scrunching up your toes or lifting them upwards in your boots as you ski. Both are responses that often lurk around long after the cause has been eradicated, blocking circulation and feedback from the snow surface. Refer to the relaxation and awareness exercises in chapters four and five if you have this problem.

Allied to the sybaritic development of heated boots, certainly one of the most helpful fitting extras over the years has been the 'orthotic': tailor-made insoles that contour the shape of the sole of the foot, provide complete contact with the whole of the base surface, support the arch and increase the quality of feedback.

Supporting the arch or even putting a small wedge under the inside heel can often remove excessive pressure on the inside ankle bone. If you have trouble standing with the skis flat on the ground, some top-of-the-line boots have canting devices or an adjustable cuff which realigns the shell for knock knees or bow legs. For more serious realignment problems take advice from an expert on canting.

SKIS

Getting to know which equipment suits you is a question of expert advice, trial and preference. Many shops have skis for testing and all reputable shops have qualified staff who can advise.

You may always hire equipment; if so, you must rely on the supplier to keep the skis well tuned. If you have your own gear, it is wise to check regularly with an expert that your skis are in top condition. My relationship with my skis is a very special one, almost a love affair, like a concert musician with his violin. To play beautiful music an instrument needs to be in tune. If you want to become a more skilful, sensitive skier you will need to keep their edges sharp and their bases waxed. Treated with respect they will respond appropriately.

Recently the ski manufacturers have realized that nearly half the skiers in the world are women and that their different physical characteristics warrant attention. A softer flex helps to initiate turns and lighter skis have appeal because they are easier to carry. Generally, more skilful women skiers prefer to stick with performance skis, choosing models with an appropriate flex pattern. Whatever you buy, take all factors into consideration and don't just be swayed by the sales patter and appearance. Please refer to chapters three and eight for more about skis.

SKI POLES

Even many advanced skiers are unaware of the difference a well-balanced, light ski pole can make to their skiing. Sadly much rental equipment is 'built to last' and heavy, unwieldy poles are often the norm. Go and feel the difference yourself in a reputable ski shop that stocks a varied range. Get to know what length you like and, if you are unsure, buy on the long side and have them cut down 1 cm (1/2 in) at a time until they feel right. As a rule, the lower arm needs to be parallel to the ground when you grasp an upturned ski pole under the basket.

CHECKLIST

This checklist will help you to include essential items when packing for your skiing holiday.

Essentials
Passport
Tickets
Money (cheques/credit cards/cash)

Clothing
Ski pants and jacket or one-piece suit
Ski socks
Thermal underwear (long johns and long-sleeved vest)
Roll-neck shirts
Sweaters
Ski gloves
Woollen ski hat
Scarf (Woollen or silk)
Après-ski boots or rubber-soled walking shoes

Equipment
Ski boots
Skis and poles (ski bag for travelling)
Small back pack
Goggles
Sunglasses
Sun cream
Lip salve
Photo for lift pass
Camera

HOW WE INTERFERE WITH OUR LEARNING AND ENJOYMENT

If our birthright is an innate ability to learn, why is it that we are unable to turn it on when we want? If all the information we need is out there waiting to be received, why can't we tune into it? It's like being a radio ham with a receiver which is perpetually mistuned or tuned into another frequency altogether!

Learning happens in fits and starts, and the rate at which we learn differs from person to person, from situation to situation. Each of us has our own unique 'learning curve' or cycle which influences the changes in our performance. Learning may be elusive at times as the brain processes and assimilates chunks of new information. You may not be ready to learn something new every day and may have to be satisfied with repeating what you already know. Most of us often have problems even doing that! How can we accelerate our learning and minimize those agonizing experiences on the plateau? By raising our awareness and avoiding potential interference. So, identify the source of the problem and take action. It could be one of the following:

Weather/snow conditions
Inappropriate terrain
Unprepared or inappropriate equipment
Other people
Lack of awareness/concentration
Unclear/unrealistic goals
Lack of enjoyment
Self-criticism/congratulation
Trying too hard
Over attachment to results
Boredom/panic
Expectations
Comparisons
Impatience
Fatigue

'Bad habits'
Habitual vocabulary
Fear/tension/anxiety

All these obstacles fall into one of two categories. They are either external or internal interference.

However much we may blame something external for poor performance or lack of enjoyment, ultimately we are responsible for how we react internally. There may be nothing we can do to change the external condition that is bothering us but we can always change our internal response.

Dan Millman in his book *The Warrior Athlete* identifies four attitudes we can adopt to deal with any situation:

RESIST

IGNORE

SURRENDER

USE

Resist means refusing to accept the reality of the situation. For example, swimming upstream against a strong current.

Ignore means refusing to acknowledge that the situation exists and perhaps putting yourself and others in danger by a lack of awareness. For example, a non-swimmer jumping into freezing water without a lifejacket or a skier going off piste without a guide.

Surrender means allowing the situation to overwhelm you. For example, a man overboard giving up fatalistically and not even attempting to swim.

Use means recognizing completely what the situation is, accepting it and using the energy within it to your advantage. For the swimmer, this means flowing with the current and using its power to reach the other side; for the skier, dancing with gravity down the slope. This principle of blending with available energy is well known in the martial arts of Aikido and T'ai Chi.

Let's have a look at the most common external and internal interferences and how we can deal with them most effectively.

WEATHER

Given that we have no influence over the weather, being properly dressed and planning to ski within reach of a cosy restaurant will help you to accept that the five-day storm is not about to abate and give you one final day of glorious sunshine. Take advantage of poor visibility to raise your awareness of subtle sensations and sounds: I have often had great fun in these conditions when I viewed them as an opportunity rather than an interference. But ignore the vagaries of the weather in the mountains at your peril. It is generally 10°C colder up the mountain than in the resort, and high-altitude wind increases the chill factor considerably.

SNOW CONDITIONS/INAPPROPRIATE TERRAIN

Difficult snow conditions and inappropriate terrain are common problems. Getting on a slope that is too difficult will inhibit progress. So be aware of where the lifts and your companions are taking you. If you find yourself in a difficult situation, you have a choice. You can view it as an opportunity to experience something new and possibly fall a lot in the process – if you are relaxed and having fun, it is unlikely that you will hurt yourself. Or you can decide you are way out of your depth and take the lift down to an easier slope – there's no shame involved and it would be much wiser than staying to get uptight and miserable.

If it has not snowed for a while or if there has been a warm spell followed by colder weather, it is likely that the snow pack on the piste will be hard or even icy. This means the ski runs may be more difficult than you expect. A red may seem like a black and a black covered in icy moguls like purgatory! Walking down is hard work and can be dangerous. If it is icy, then side-stepping with skis that can grip over a longer length is wiser than taking off your skis and trying to grip in ski boots.

UNPREPARED OR INAPPROPRIATE EQUIPMENT

How often do we blame our gear for our poor performance? 'If only I had better skis . . . sharper edges . . . shorter ski poles . . .' Unsuitable or ill-prepared equipment can cause untold misery but, having seen miracles performed on the most antiquated and beaten-up gear, I suspect that some people wallow in their excuses. Be honest. If the equipment is at fault, sort it out! If it isn't at fault, recognize that you are not taking responsibility for your performance.

OTHER PEOPLE

When you feel freaked out by other people skiing too close, ask yourself the following questions: 'Did I check the slope for a gap in the flow of people before setting off?'; 'Where am I looking?'; 'Am I seeing the spaces on the slope or have I only got other people in my sights?' Since we tend to go where we look, it is useful to recognize that we are often responsible for 'attracting' a crowd!

Wild skiers are certainly distracting. However if we react to this interference by getting uptight, it will only exacerbate the problem. By letting go of tension, raising awareness of route finding and developing peripheral vision we can blend and flow with others on the slope. We have an innate problem-solving capacity that will cope with unforeseen obstacles and make adjustments to a previously planned route.

LACK OF AWARENESS/CONCENTRATION

This is *the* great inhibitor and one that we will be addressing throughout this book. If you aren't fully present, your body and brain don't stand a chance of learning how to ski. Many of the exercises and games are designed to help you to let go of the mental activity that prevents you from being fully present by giving you something more useful to focus on. I urge you to participate 100%.

UNCLEAR/UNREALISTIC GOALS

Being unclear about what we want or having unrealistic goals are the next two best ways of inhibiting our own learning. We have already covered this topic in chapter two but it is worth reminding you again!

LACK OF ENJOYMENT

If you aren't having fun, take a few moments to identify what is getting in the way of your enjoyment. We can't expect to be ecstatic all the time but there is no reason to stay in the doldrums for long. Learning seems to happen most frequently when we are relaxed and enjoying ourselves so keep your eye on your fun meter. Keep yourself interested in what you are doing by getting involved in one of the games in chapters five and six. Our natural state is one of playfulness, and like a child we can be cajoled out of a mood if our interest is stimulated.

SELF-CRITICISM

Much of our self-critical chatter is unfounded and stems from a poor self-image (see chapter six). The rest is the type of self-castigation that results from making a mistake. *It is crucial to recognize that making errors is a natural part of the learning process. Sadly we have learned to view mistakes as 'bad' or 'wrong'. By labelling them in this way we actually stop ourselves learning. Every error we make is essential feedback if the body is to recognize what works and what doesn't so it can make the necessary corrections.*

By judging and turning our backs on our errors we deny

ourselves greater awareness. Saying 'that was a bad turn' tells us nothing. By using focused awareness, we can help our bodies. Saying 'I was only 70 per cent committed to that turn, missed the pole plant and ended with hip rotation' tells us something useful. *What we resist persists; we will tend to repeat the same error again and again unless we bring it into consciousness.*

We aren't perfect all the time! Severe judgements inhibit learning; be patient and allow your body to make the necessary corrections. In the awareness exercises receive all the input and feedback non-judgementally, i.e. as pure information without any 'add on' opinions, good/bad values or labels. It may take a little while to get out of the habit of continually judging everything you do, and you will probably find yourself judging yourself for judging! You will be surprised how liberating non-judgemental awareness is.

SELF-CONGRATULATION

This is the converse of self-criticism. How many times have you congratulated yourself on something only to go splat! What is the old saying, 'Pride comes before a fall'? Once again the self-talk distracts us. Review your run afterwards by all means but see it for what it was. Too often we focus on the only turn that really worked or the only turn that didn't and so we distort our perception of our real ability. Seeing clearly the truth about our skiing, its strong points and its weaknesses, will bring us closer to transforming it.

TRYING TOO HARD

Trying too hard wastes energy, creates unnecessary tension and interferes with muscle movement. Trying hard stems from self-doubt. If we were trusting in our ability we would just go ahead and act without additional effort. To show you how we desensitize ourselves by trying, select two objects of similar but unequal weight. Hold one in each hand. Grip them tightly and weigh them up. Which is heavier and which is lighter? Now relax your hold and notice how much easier it is to feel the difference, how you are much more sensitive when there is no unnecessary tension.

I remember once working with a professional tennis player and asking him to focus on different parts of his body as he was serving. He found he was using all sorts of muscles in his jaw, shoulders, arms and legs that did not have to be working when he made contact with the ball. He was amazed that by 'trying too hard' he had set up so much inefficiency and wasted energy. Eventually, he was able to regroove his serve without the habitual extra tension and was delighted with the added consistency and fluidity of his movements. The effect was startling as he released greater power at the crucial moment of contact.

It is interesting that the word 'try' actually suggests a lack of commitment. Trying implies possible failure. 'I'll try to do it' is different from 'I'll do it'. 'I'll try to do it' is frequently followed by failure and 'well, I tried' as if that were some justification. Notice when you use these words. Recognize the cop-out inherent within them and the lack of commitment or clarity of intention. Just by changing your vocabulary you will influence that negative mind-set.

OVER ATTACHMENT TO RESULTS

We need to have goals and the intention to achieve them but if we are overly concerned about achieving results we will inhibit our progress. This over attachment stems from being dependent on results for our sense of self-worth, from seeking approval through achievements in external activities either from oneself or from others.

Our worth cannot be measured by our talent because it is beyond measure. Once we recognize that, if our goal is clearly defined and realistic we can let go of over attachment to results. When we are free to make mistakes and to fail, we are able to learn and are more likely to succeed. There need be no worries about whether we are going to achieve results or not. So, paradoxically, when we let go of trying hard to acheive we move closer to our goal.

BOREDOM VERSUS PANIC

Ultimately it is the mountain that is the teacher. Its slopes face us with a variety of choices: flat, sloping or sheer. Our response to these different slope angles will range from boredom to panic, depending upon the conditions at the time and our perception of our ability. It is useful for the purposes of learning and improving performance to recognize how you respond and notice when you are verging on the extremes.

Neither boredom nor panic zones are useful states for learning. The mental activity in both extremes prevents us from fully experiencing the present. The 'comfort zone' is the one in which you can receive maximum feedback from the environment without any stress interfering. The 'stretch zone' is your next goal, the situation you have to face in order to progress. The ideal in terms of progress is for a perceived stretch zone to become a new comfort zone and so on.

Some people tend to get stuck in either comfort or stretch zones. Check it out. Are you someone who never takes a risk and always skis on blue runs? Or are you the sort of skier who is constantly out of your depth, on the edge of control and perpetually high on adrenalin? Neither of these types will make steady progress; we need to balance stretch with comfort and comfort with stretch.

Choose your terrain with utmost care. Ski where you can be relaxed and happy. Once you feel confidence and competence, you can add a little 'stretch' to extend your ability. Then go back to where you feel comfortable. That way you will learn to flow with gravity and increase your speed or slope angle without interfering with your posture and balance.

EXPECTATIONS

Expectations of what should or is likely to happen often get in the way of our progress. They distort our perception of what is actually happening and rob us of the truth. It's rather like having a tint in your glasses and assuming the world will look the same when you take them off. Expectations that are too high will produce disappointment as you compare what you think *ought* to be happening with what is *actually* happening. On the other hand, expectations that are too low tend to be self-fulfilling prophecies. Recognizing expectations, letting go of them and opening yourself to what is happening will help you to make the most of your time on the slopes.

COMPARISONS

Rates of progress fluctuate. Beware of comparing your learning with someone else's or expecting to learn at the same rate as you did yesterday.

IMPATIENCE

Practice makes perfect. Perfect practice makes perfect sooner and perfect practice with *awareness and patience* makes perfect even faster. Be patient with yourself, as you would with a little child learning to walk. Would you tick him off and tell him to hurry up and get it 'right'?! If you make a mistake, smile at yourself. It works wonders.

FATIGUE

If you do not prepare yourself adequately for skiing you can expect to feel tired in the mountains. Even without the physical demands of skiing, you will be breathing harder to compensate for the lack of oxygen in the air at higher altitudes. Combine this with several hours of travel, alcohol, the excitement and effort of getting on the slopes and the mid-week blues are certain to strike. Fatigue is at the root of many injuries and interferes with enjoyment and progress. Here are some tips to keep you at your best:

- ** Keep an eye on your energy level. Stop before you reach fatigue, not after.
- ** Pace yourself the first few days so that you avoid depleting your energy resources.
- ** Eat plenty of carbohydrates, e.g. pasta, bread, rice and potatoes.
- ** Eat a high-energy breakfast, e.g. muesli and/or bread.
- ** Take dried fruit and nuts with you rather than chocolate. Beware of the short-term energy 'high' of sugar.
- ** Drink plenty of water. Exercise and breathing in a dry atmosphere dehydrate the body. Avoid coffee and alcohol, which deplete body fluids rather than add to them.

If you find you are still unable to get involved in what is going on, and fatigue is not the cause, you can be sure that your mind is getting in the way. There is always something valuable to be gained from the doldrums. Even though you may feel miserable, recognize that you have an opportunity to learn something rather than a problem.

> *There is no such thing as a problem without a gift for you in its hands. You seek problems because you need their gifts.*

> *What the caterpillar calls the end of the world, the master calls a butterfly.*

Richard Bach

(*Illusions*)

BAD HABITS

'Bad' habits are simply patterns of movements that are ineffective or inefficient. They are usually areas of unawareness: movement patterns in which we are not fully conscious of what we are doing. Often you only know you have a habit because someone has pointed it out to you, or perhaps, as you become more sensitive as you ski, you may have noticed yourself.

The only cure for a habit is to really feel it, to become aware of it.

Each time you repeat a habit you groove it deeper in your memory. By exaggerating the movement you will raise awareness of it and then doing the opposite can help break the pattern. As you repattern with awareness, the movement may feel strange. But when muscle memory increases and learning takes place this awkwardness will disappear and the new will become familiar and comfortable. Habits give us the illusion of comfort. *Awareness cuts through illusion so you may feel that you are getting worse before you get better.*

HABITUAL VOCABULARY

The language we habitually use is a powerful influence on what we experience. It is valuable to become aware of the words that unconsciously programme our negative behaviour-patterns and change them for words that support our learning process.

> *Difficult* (means 'I'm likely to fail') change to *challenging*.
> *Problem* (as above) change to *opportunity*.
> *I can't* (means 'I won't') change to *I can and will*.
> *I'll try to do* (means 'I'll probably fail') change to *I'll do*.
> *Bad/good* (not useful in terms of feedback) change to *efficient/inefficient* or *effective/ineffective*.
> *I should/ought to* (means 'I have no choice') change to *I could*.

This last one transformed my life. I would lie in bed in the morning saying, 'I should get up' every five minutes and resisting it. When I changed it to 'I could get up' I had a choice – 'I will or I won't get up now' – and put that way I usually did!

FEAR, THE GREAT INHIBITOR

By far the most common interference in skiing is fear and its close relatives, anxiety and tension. Fear can become your best friend rather than your worst enemy if you simply get to know it better. It is after all a response that has kept our species from being consumed by predators and unharmed by other threats. In our macho society we are often frightened of admitting that we are afraid. However, it is the most common inhibitor in every situation and at every level of expertise. Since we tend to deny its existence, we are often unaware that we carry many unconscious fears and that our past history of unexpressed fears is embedded in our posture and movements.

You may be surprised to hear that even expert skiers experience anxiety from time to time. It is not something that disappears once you have mastered your skis, although its threshold changes as confidence develops. The initial fear response is very similar to the pleasant buzz of exhilaration so it is worth checking whether you are misinterpreting the butterflies in your stomach. It is after all the rush of adrenalin that prepares us for action. Excitement and fear are so closely related that if you find skiing exhilarating, it is likely you will seek that thrill in a slightly steeper slope or a faster speed. This will bring you closer to your personal borderline between calculated risk and danger. So be attentive!

HOW HOLDING BACK INTERFERES WITH BALANCING

As soon as we experience fear in a situation, however slight, there is a tendency to hold back, to withdraw. This interferes fundamentally with our ability to move and to balance effectively. The effect is often felt first in the feet, when curled toes try desperately to get a grip on Mother Earth. However slight and unconscious the response, the body moves back slightly, perhaps by only millimetres at the base, but the effect further up the structure and on the centre of mass is substantial. Another symptom of fear is the overly straight lower leg which has gone rigid in a defensive action. The classic *position toilette* is the extreme response to fear. Here the whole body distorts by rocking back onto the heels, drawing back the elbows and hollowing the lower spine.

Whatever the degree of 'holding back', and some skiers are unaware that it is going on, the imbalance that is set up has to find compensation. The initial negative response and the necessary compensation both use energy, constantly draining the supply. Other muscles in different parts of the body have to react to correct balance. Frequently the result is burning thighs and an inability to respond 'athletically'. It is rather like trying to drive the car from the back seat.

It is crucial in learning to ski that we minimize this defensive holding back or the patterns of movement learned will always contain an element of imbalance and inefficiency.

THE SOURCE OF FEAR

As children we were told, 'be careful', 'watch out', 'no, don't do that' and 'you'll hurt yourself'. True, our elders were often warning us of dangers that we could not conceptualize, but the underlying communication that we received was that we were not able to cope with whatever we were about to undertake.

This conditioned echo of self-doubt reverberates whenever we are about to take a risk. Fundamentally we do not believe that we are equipped to handle whatever situation presents itself. Self-doubt is the source of all our irrational fears. Some fears are quite unconscious, early imprints on our circuitry that surface without our conscious awareness. By exploring our physical responses we can bring unconscious fears into consciousness and then let go of them.

> *It is not that you must be free from fear. The moment you try to free yourself from fear, you create a resistance against fear. Resistance in any form does not end fear.*
>
> *What is needed rather than a running away or controlling or suppressing or any other resistance, is understanding fear; that means, watch it, learn about it, come directly into contact with it.*
>
> *We are to learn about fear, not how to escape from it, not how to resist it through courage and so on.*

J. Krishnamurti

THE FEAR RESPONSE

The physical symptoms of anxiety vary considerably from a barely perceptible catch in breath to more obvious sweaty palms, dry mouth, muscular tension, cold feet and body trembling. The more extreme responses to fear are a pounding heart, muscular rigidity, hair raising and petrifying panic. These reactions to what we perceive as danger fall into two categories: *the response that enables and the response that disables.*

The instinctive response that enables is the innate fight or flight mechanism which equips us to deal with an immediate and *real* danger. This is truly a state of fearlessness. Examples include escaping from the charging bull or saving the drowning man, when the adrenalin released into the blood stream sets off a series of reactions in the body to provide greater perceptual abilities and energy to assist survival. The pupils dilate, the heart beats faster, the breathing quickens and time seems to slow down. There is clarity and decisiveness; the immediate and real danger is met with courage and conviction. In order to stay in one piece we need to discriminate between imagined fear and our response to a genuine threat to our survival.

The response that disables is closely associated with the mental constructs of self-doubt and self-chatter. If we think that something sinister or life threatening is going to happen in the future, our bodies react by creating the sensations of fear but without the appropriate release. The heart pumps but there is no actual flight, no dive into the deep. Instead there is an increased sensation of hesitation, of holding back – as muscles tighten and breathing becomes more constricted, creating physical imbalance. Our perception becomes distorted as we narrow our focus onto the very thing we are wanting to avoid. Our self-doubt has disabled us, inhibiting a natural, active, balanced response to the current situation.

Fear to let fall a drop and you spill a lot.

Malay proverb.

After having a skiing injury I had my first confrontation with abnormal fear. By the time I got to the lift in the morning I would feel exhausted by all the mental activity and tension in my body. The fear was burning fuel fast. Feeling weak and helpless, I became more afraid of the fear itself than of hurting myself again. As my mind created all sorts of scenarios, I can vividly recollect that sinking feeling, a sadness that the sport I had loved so much had become so painful. At that time I thought that 'losing one's nerve' was a permanent state of affairs.

> *There is nothing to fear but fear itself.*
>
> Theodore Roosevelt

By distinguishing between reality and illusion, between actual and imagined danger, we can start to take charge of what may seem to be beyond our conscious control. One of the side effects of fear is the feeling of powerlessness, of having no choice, and its consequence is to keep our fear alive. If you want to, you can turn your fear into power.

A CLOSER LOOK AT FEAR

We come into the world with only one innate fear, that of falling, and all the subsequent fears we experience are learned. There are several fears and all seem valid when we are caught up by them, however irrational on consideration. Fear of injury, of failure, of looking foolish, of losing control and of the unknown are the most common in skiing.

Human imagination seems to excel in creating fantasies of what could go wrong. Some hilarious and completely impossible situations become fixed as a reality in our minds. What of the beginner who is convinced he is going to fall off the mountain and arrive splat on the valley floor? Such marvellous constructs of our imagination! Don't laugh; you have probably got a few yourself. How about these?

    **   'If I fall over and break my leg, I'll lose my job, not be able to pay the mortgage and my wife will leave me for that fellow with the fast car.'

    **   'If I ski well and show them how competent I really am, then they will expect me to do well in the race and I'm not sure I could handle that.'

**   'If I make a hash of this, she'll think I'm a wimp . . .'

**   'If I don't keep up, he'll get angry and I'll be left behind in future.'

**   'If I fall on that patch of ice, I am bound to hurt myself.'

THE PARADOX OF FEAR

There is a strange paradox here. What we are most afraid of we tend to attract like a magnet. When I was first learning to ski off piste in the trees, I kept falling down the holes by their trunks and getting inextricably tangled in branches and covered in snow. After pulling me out feet first for the second time, my companion asked me where I was looking while skiing. I replied, 'At the trees, of course. I'm afraid of hitting them and getting stuck.' Laughter. Then: 'you may find looking for the spaces between the trees more helpful!' It seemed so obvious when I considered it, and from then on I started looking at where I wanted to go, rather than where I didn't. The eyes tend to lead us where we look so if the mind focuses on an ice patch or an obstacle the next thing we know is we are on top of it.

If we have visions of disaster, with the imbalance that these thoughts set up, we create just the situations that we wish to avoid. This downward spiral is fuelled further by our 'I told you so' reaction when the worst has just happened so completing the vicious circle.

POWER VERSUS PARALYSIS

Our fears are not usually about what is happening now, in the present. They are projections of future events or memories of past events with accompanying 'I told you so's' to fuel their realism. They may be just occasional doubts that are thrust aside for more positive dreams or they may be varieties of recurring self-chatter that are listened to and believed.

Once these thoughts put down roots and grow they are harder to uproot but it is never impossible. It just takes some commitment, trust and awareness. You may have convinced yourself that you are powerless, incapable of skiing a certain way on a certain slope or in certain conditions. It may be that you have a negative self-image that fuels these thoughts and you will have to spend time recreating a more positive one. (Refer to chapter six for more on self-image.)

Fear tends to paralyse, blocking both enjoyment and learning. The reverse of fear is power, power to choose how you feel and not be the brunt of your emotions.

SOME TRUTHS ABOUT FEAR

** Everybody experiences some level of fear in their life. It is a great comfort to realize that we are not alone in experiencing fear; even expert skiers have moments of anxiety.

** Recognize the difference between real danger and imagined fear. Is the mythical snow snake biting your leg right now?

** There is nothing 'wrong' with fear. Just ask yourself whether it is effective or not. Remember that an appropriate sense of caution will keep you alive in the mountains.

** Realize that it is *you* making *you* tense; take responsibility for it.

** The initial fear response is a sign of being ready for action. Act.

** Fear will never go away on its own. There is no way to get rid of fear without experiencing whatever it is that makes you afraid. Fear will not go away before you ski that slope, only after.

** It may be some consolation to hear that pushing through the fear is easier than living with the dread that you are going to be confronted by it.

WHAT CAN WE DO ABOUT IT?

Whether you are gripped by fear or only occasionally anxious, you can add a great deal more to your skiing by paying attention to the following:

** Decide to regain your power.

** Acknowledge the self-chatter and get to know your particular fears.

** Spend time uncovering the body tension related to your fear.

** Feel the fear and do it anyway.

** Learn to welcome adrenalin.

** Begin self-trust reinforcement.

** Do relaxation and breathing exercises.

Decide to regain your power. First you have to decide that you do not want to be at the mercy of your fears any more. The reward is a release of energy that can be put to constructive use.

Acknowledge the self-chatter and get to know your particular fears. Recognize the self-talk for what it is, a fantasy, and identify exactly what it is you are afraid of. As you get to know what triggers the downward spiral, you can start dealing with the first signs rather than letting it take control.

Spend time uncovering the body tension related to your fear. Do a body check when you next go skiing. Choose an easy slope. As you ski become aware of your body, working systematically from the head down. Let the unnecessary tension speak to you. Give it a chance; it is probably by now very familiar and may even 'feel comfortable'. When you have discovered an area (mine is either my hands, arms, feet or stomach) focus on it. Where is it exactly? How big is it? Rate it on a scale of 0 to 10. Stay with it and let it go. To keep your attention on the tension call out the numbers corresponding to your tension every few seconds. If you 'stare at it' for long enough, it will begin to disappear.

Feel the fear and do it anyway. Given that your fear is unrealistic, acknowledge its energy and invite it to join you while you tackle whatever it is that you are afraid of together.

Learn to welcome adrenalin. Once you get to recognize that the rush of adrenalin is in fact a signal to act, welcome it as a friend that is there to help you perform beyond your perceived limits.

Begin self-trust reinforcement. To reinforce a more appropriate response within your subconscious, start to see yourself doing what you are afraid of in your mind's eye. There is no danger, no risk, no reason to fear anything. Allow yourself to ski with freedom and joy. Begin repeating an affirmation. (Please refer to chapter six for an explanation of visualization and affirmations.)

Do relaxation and breathing exercises. Our breath is the link between the body and the mind. When the mind is disturbed, the breathing is bound to be 'uptight'– high *up* in the chest and *tight*. By allowing the breathing to return to a more normal pattern the mind will become calm and quiet. In focusing on your breathing you bring your attention back into the present. Anxiety is that gap between the now and the future. Come back to the *now*. You can still look down the slope that frightened you. The difference is you are including the future in the here and now rather than projecting yourself out into the future and losing your sense of being in the present.

DEALING WITH SPECIFIC FEARS

Fear of falling

If falling over is what you fear most, then learning to ski is going to be a painful process. Trying not to fall over will just set up the conditions for what you are most afraid of. Skiing *is* a form of falling. Every time you flow with gravity you are surrendering to this possibility. So either quit or get used to falling! I spent so long resisting falling in freestyle competitions that when I began free skiing again I had forgotten that falling is 'allowed'. Falling is 'natural' and falling, when the body and mind are relaxed, is 'fun' and usually *painless*. Falling only hurts on really hard slopes and when one stiffens and resists the inevitable.

The way to cure a fear of falling is to fall, again and again. When I realized that falling was no big deal, I spent the whole day looking for excuses to roll about in the snow. My skiing reached a peak that day too – relaxed and flowing as never before. Obviously soft snow feels better than hard pack, so go and find yourself a patch and let yourself go. Do this without skis as a slow, twisting fall can test even the best bindings. First just sit down in the snow and feel its softness. Then learn how to fall so that when it does happen it is not an unknown quantity. Remember how much fun it was to fall and roll in sand or snow as a child? Learn to straighten your legs as you fall to protect the vulnerable knee joints which damage more easily when bent. Learn to wrap and roll, going with a fall without sticking out your arms and inviting injury to shoulders, thumbs and wrists.

While you are doing this, ask yourself what is it that I am really afraid of? Of hurting myself, of failing, of looking foolish or of the unknown?

Fear of Injury

There is no denying that skiing involves some risk of injury to soft tissue or bones. If you are terrified of harming yourself or cannot afford to be immobilized then perhaps a more sedentary sport would be appropriate. However, the main culprit in most injuries is the rigidity that fear creates in resisting a fall. The expression 'I have hurt myself' contains more truth than we may realize! So weigh up the risks, make a decision about whether you are willing to accept them and then let go of your fear.

Fear of the Unknown

> *As a rule what is out of sight disturbs men's minds more seriously than what they see.*
>
> Julius Caesar

For some people a fear of falling is actually a fear of the unknown. If life has not included contact sports, falling off a horse or other opportunities to learn how to tumble and roll, then the one way to overcome this is to find out that the fear is more frightening than the actual falling. This seems to be true for all fears of the unknown, so identify what it is that is bothering you, acknowledge the anxiety and bring yourself back into the present. Only when you are experiencing the present will you be able to respond more appropriately to whatever it is that frightens you.

Fear of failure

It is a fact that in learning anything we are bound to make mistakes. Even little children, the expert learners, don't get everything right first time. If we were afraid of failure at that age, I wonder how we would ever learn to walk and talk?

We learn to fear failure as we get older, as the results of our actions take on greater and greater importance. The requirement to achieve separates us from the task at hand. It may be that the opinions of others matter a great deal, that their approval, is sought and disapproval avoided at all costs or that we demand personal personal perfection to bolster a wobbly self-image. Whatever the motive, this overattachment to achieving results divorces us from the harmony of the activity, inhibiting receptivity and feedback.

Fear of looking foolish

The fear of looking foolish is a close relative of the fear of failure. In this version the ego is interested in maintaining 'face' at all costs. In pursuit of this end experience will be denied, fun avoided and learning inhibited – just in case I make a fool of myself'.

It is easy to crack this amongst a group of friends – with my clients we play all sorts of silly games with no purpose other than to laugh at ourselves and each other. Acting out animals or imitating each other's idiosyncracies or skiiing in the most uncoordinated way we can imagine. Anything that gives us permission to break through the restrictions of fearing how we look in the eyes of others. After doing this, there is a freedom of expression within the group that allows for experimentation and learning to take place. The energy that was once consumed by self-interest has been liberated and is now redirected towards mutual support and encouragement. Many people describe this as a turning point in letter go of their self-imposed limitations.

Fear of Success

Strange as it may seem, the fear of success can be as terrifying as the fear of failure. Sometimes it feels easier just to stumble around and stay out of the limelight. We can trick ourselves into mediocre performance by fearing our potential. 'You mean I can do anything I set my heart on? Oh! Goodness me, then I wouldn't have any excuses next time!' The truth is that our unused capacity *is* staggering. Each time we withdraw from an opportunity to grow we deny our potential.

RELAXATION EXERCISE

Make sure that you are warmly and comfortably dressed and free from disturbances. Lie on your back on a firm bed or on the floor. You might want to cover yourself with a rug since the body temperature will drop as the metabolism slows down.

1. Pay attention to your breathing and follow the air in and out of your lungs. Let your breath flow in and fill you and flow out freely. Allow the inhale and the exhale to balance so that they are the same length.

2. When you feel ready, pay attention to your toes and feet. Inhale and slowly tighten the muscles, hold for a moment and then let go as you exhale. Feel the tension melting away, leaving your toes and feet feeling heavy and warm. Breathe deeply and relax. If you feel any residual tension, repeat the tightening and releasing in rhythm with your breathing.

3. Now bring your attention slowly up your legs, inhaling and tensing and exhaling and releasing. Notice the different muscles and become familiar with the heavy, warm, relaxed feeling as you release the tension.

4. Carry on upwards through your body to your buttocks, lower back, stomach, rib cage, shoulders, arms and hands.

5. Inhale and screw up your face and tighten your jaw; exhale and release. Check that your jaw is loose and your tongue is relaxed in your mouth.

6. Do a body scan to feel if there is any remaining tension.

7. Enjoy this relaxed state for a few minutes. When you are ready to get up, wriggle your toes and fingers, open your eyes, bend your knees, bringing your heels towards your buttocks, and roll over onto your side before getting up. Do this slowly and with a new awareness of your relaxed body.

8. Keep this awareness of your body with you as you move and let go of unnecessary tension as it arises.

TENSION-RELEASE EXERCISE

If you are sitting or standing, do a body scan systematically from the head down and notice if there are any areas of tension. Common areas are neck and shoulders, hands, stomach, buttocks and feet. Let your body tell you where the tension is. Do the following release process on each area in turn:

1. Identify the area of tension. Feel its dimension and density.

2. Put your attention into this area and simply observe it. You may find that it starts to dissipate of its own accord. Breathe away the tension. Exhale and let it go.

3. If it persists, rate it on a scale of 0 to 10 with 10 being maximum tension.

4. Every few seconds check what number the tension corresponds to. It may increase slightly before it decreases.

5. Alternatively, you may find using colours helpful. This method is particularly effective if you have a tension headache. Feel the tension; see what size, shape and colour it is.

6. Every few seconds ask yourself, 'What size is it now?' . . . 'What shape is it now?'. . .'What colour is it now?' Allow the tension to change size, shape and colour until it becomes transparent and invisible.

You can do a complete body scan in this way at any time during the day. If you practise this exercise before you go skiing, you will find it easier to use on the slopes. As you become more sensitive to your body it will become easier to notice tension as it arises and deal with it immediately rather than let it build up.

Please refer to chapter seven for more about breathing and deep relaxation. Get into the habit of doing a short tension-release exercise before you set off down the slopes.

STIFLING A YAWN

Of course, you don't want to be so relaxed that you want to lie down and go to sleep. Get to know from your own experience what works for you, what is your 'optimum arousal' level. You may be someone who responds to stress by being 'under-aroused'. The symptoms are yawning and lack of interest. If this is true for you, you need to discover ways of 'psyching' yourself up. By getting yourself physically moving you can counteract some of this inertia.

Singing a rousing song or mental imagery of some dynamic symbol will also work wonders. (See chapter six for an explanation of mental imagery.) Adapt the following exercise for your needs and create a dynamic, energizing resource.

THIRTY-NINE STEPS

When I used to compete in the freestyle aerial event I used to get very afraid. Having a vivid imagination does not help when it runs away and fantasizes about all the ghastly things that could happen. I could usually land on my feet after a front or back somersault, but not always the first time off a new jump. Each competition was held in a different resort, on a jump built on slopes that had variable in-run angles, different transition lengths and jump profiles. At each competition the first jump was a nailbiting affair.

I would slip quietly away from the crowd, close my eyes and imagine taking my dog for a walk down the garden and onto the beach. Somehow I intuited that this mental process would help me to feel calm. Focusing on each of the thirty-nine steps leading from the garden to the beach was crucial. Each one was different and my attention was completely focused on not missing a step. Then I would go back into the competition arena in a calm, focused state, able to see more clearly, feel my speed in the in-run and sense where I was in the air.

Since then I have discovered that this sort of visualization process is practised by many athletes. Here are some guidelines so that you can create your own special place that you can retreat to when feeling particularly uptight:

1. First clarify for yourself what sort of quality you would like to assume. For example, you may want to feel 'calm and serene' or 'competent and in charge' or 'energized and dynamic'.

2. Recall from your own experience a place or situation in which you express that and feel at one with that quality. Let's assume that you would like to feel 'competent and in charge' so pick a situation in which that is true for you. You may be an expert at something or in charge of something at work or feel this way when driving your car.

3. Recall as much detail as possible how your body feels when you are in charge, how your voice sounds when speaking from this position of strength, how clearly you see the situation.

4. What key word or words describe you now? For example: 'I am calm'; 'I feel strong', 'I am able' or 'I am dynamic'.

5. Repeat the words to yourself.

6. Now come back to the present, bringing with you all those positive feelings to apply to the situation at hand.

7. Trust yourself to respond appropriately.

8. Repeat the key word to yourself to focus your mind and reinforce positive feelings.

Having set the scene for learning, performing and enjoying skiing, we now need to examine more closely how we can maximize the necessary input by raising awareness of our bodies, equipment and environment.

Chapter Five

Balancing and the senses

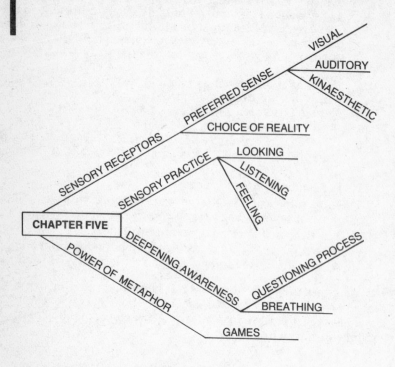

CHOOSING OUR REALITY

We would have no idea of our whereabouts if we did not take in information through sensory receptors. Our senses let us know what is 'out there'. By tasting, smelling, touching, hearing, seeing and feeling, the brain creates a multi-dimensional sensory image of 'reality'. To save ourselves from being overwhelmed by unnecessary detail, the brain and sense organs tend to be selective and much of what is going on is ignored. Even so, we unconsciously absorb a massive amount of sensory information in our everyday habitual activities and often are only conscious of variations on the norm.

Right now when I pay attention to the sounds around me, I can hear the hum of the refrigerator, the wind in the wisteria, a clock ticking, a car passing, a bird singing and the sound the keys of my word processor make when I press them. Oh yes, and a sigh as I wonder what to say next. If I am focused on those words, the peripheral sounds recede and my attention becomes selective.

It is the same when we look. There's a huge amount to take in. I can focus in on one object or expand my vision to include more than 180 degrees. We tend to see what we are most interested in, or afraid of, choosing our outlook, our view of reality. There are virtually limitless ways of seeing the same scene by simply choosing a theme. For example, by selecting a colour or comparing relationships of objects to one another we can alter our perception.

Likewise what we feel is influenced by our choice of focus and interest. There's nothing like boredom to highlight an uncomfortable chair or deciding that we got out of the wrong side of the bed to draw all the possible negativities around us into sharp focus.

Interestingly research indicates that we only use about 50 per cent of all our senses. When one sense is lost, it is possible to compensate by developing the remaining senses – as in a blind person's heightened sense of touch and hearing.

So our awareness is shaped by what we choose to focus on and we get into habits, both conscious and unconscious, acting automatically in a pattern of learned responses. What may work quite well for us in our daily activities might not be adequate when skiing down a mountain.

MAKING SENSE

In a dog's world, smells rate pretty highly and can often dominate sounds or sights. One day my dog chased a rabbit round and round a large gorse bush. After a couple of circuits, the rabbit suddenly broke away and, even though plainly visible to me, the dog carried on rushing round the bush with his nose glued to the scent.

Studies indicate that we too have a preferred or dominant reference frame through which we receive and recall information. These internal representations of the world are either visual, auditory or kinaesthetic (our 'feeling sense') and vary from person to person. (No doubt someone who has developed an extraordinary ability for differentiating between tastes or smells may be an exception to this rule.) The dominant system is backed up by the others and may vary in different activities.

Some indication of whether you process information primarily through visual pictures, sounds or feelings can be gleaned from listening to the words you use to describe your 'world', from whether you have artistic, musical or athletic talent or from the ease with which you receive input through your various senses. The extreme examples would be the artist who finds great ease in processing information through his eyes, forming pictures in his mind and whose language may include many pictorial words and phrases such as 'perspective', 'the way I see it' or 'looking at it this way'. The musician who is sensitive to every sound and even hears music in the splatter of raindrops may use expressions like, 'Yes, I hear you', 'it sounds as if' and 'that rings a bell'. The athlete or dancer who is kinaesthetically dominant easily gets the feel for any movement and is likely to 'to get to grips with', 'have the feeling that' or 'grasp that'.

Understanding which system you favour may throw some light on situations in your past when you felt that you were not on the same 'wavelength' as somebody or couldn't see 'eye to eye'. It could even have been your ski instructor, explaining something that made sense to him but not to you! Let's be invisible spectators, watching a typical scenario in the mountains. Can you spot the mismatch in communication?

> INSTRUCTOR: (Suntanned, leaning on ski poles) You must feel ze resistance with your feet.
>
> CLIENT: (Looking perplexed) What?
>
> INSTRUCTOR: Push against ze big toe. Understand?
>
> CLIENT: I just can't picture it . . .
>
> INSTRUCTOR: Get a feel of pressure, ya?
>
> CLIENT: I don't see what you mean. Please show me again.
>
> INSTRUCTOR: Vat must I do to have you grasp zis?
>
> CLIENT: Oh dear, I'm listening as hard as I can but I just can't

make sense of what you are telling me. Let me look at it again, please.

They may never make sense of each other and become more and more frustrated. The fact that he was using only 'feeling' words severely limited his ability to communicate. Hopefully, she will see what he is doing in his demonstrations and copy the shapes he is making, letting go of his words, which only confuse her. He will probably just shrug his shoulders – after all his English was word perfect.

Their dilemma is a classic mismatch. This sort of confusion arises when two people are attempting to communicate but are using words which create unfamiliar internal representations of the message. To 'talk the same language as someone' is not just about using English or French. It is about using the type of words that will gain access to the way someone processes information internally.

The enlightened teacher can tune into students and 'match' them either by reading the verbal and physical clues as to how they operate internally or by repeating everything in three ways so that one style will connect with the experience of each client. Once a connection is created, then the learner can be encouraged to develop the 'weaker' systems and senses. As your own coach you must tune into your own processing system. By raising awareness of your own sensory strengths and weaknesses you can develop your less dominant senses. You will also be able to convert an instruction which may first appear as empty words into something that has meaning – into something that makes sense.

The following exercise will help you to find out which is your preferred representational system. Read though the lists and notice which of the three is the easiest to evoke and which is the hardest. Make a note.

VISUAL

Close your eyes and practise forming the following images in your mind's eye. If you cannot see colour (some people cannot at first), just see the shapes in black and white.

The Swiss flag (a white cross on red)

A blue circle on white

The cover of this book

A ski slope with skiers

   A friend's face

AUDITORY
Close your eyes and recreate the following sounds:
   A car passing . . . getting louder and quieter
   Birds singing and the wind in the trees
   Your skis on the snow
   Someone calling your name
   A piece of music

KINAESTHETIC (touch, feeling and body awareness)
Close your eyes and feel yourself doing the following movements:
   Shaking someone's hand
   Riding a bicycle or swimming
   Skiing on easy terrain
   Doing up your ski boots
   Another favourite physical activity

If you found one of the representational systems difficult to recreate, it is likely that you do not receive much of this type of input from the outside world. By tuning into such information and learning to include more of it in your everyday activities you will become more open to receiving this input when skiing.

SENSORY PRACTICE

The key to deepening your experience through your senses is to ask yourself specific questions about the situations in which you find yourself. You can practise this in any activity. Your mind may say it is impossible to take in so many details, and it is right! The thinking mind cannot process this sort of information. Let your senses receive the information and allow your subconscious to do the processing without comment or analysis.

Seeing

There is a world of difference between having good eyesight and having visual skill. Visual skill is the ability of the brain to interpret accurately the information received via the eye. Whereas eyesight cannot generally be improved, visual skills can.

We actually see at the back of our heads and not at the front as it seems. An area at the back of the brain deals with the input from the eyes and forms the images that we assume are out there. If the muscles of the eye are not coordinated, there can be inaccuracies and a distortion of the facts. Notice how your eyes move as you follow these words on the page.

Now look up and take in your surroundings. Close your eyes and re-create that image in your mind. Open your eyes again, look up and really examine everything, shifting your focus continually. Observe relationships, colour, texture, patterns, light and shade. Now close your eyes and re-create the image. How much more were you able to see this time? You may notice inaccuracies in your recalled image so make corrections. Do this exercise as often as you like in unfamiliar surroundings and develop your ability to see.

In skiing, particularly when starting to ski faster, we need to notice the lie of the whole slope as well as the undulations and bumps of the immediate terrain. In the USSR astronauts are trained on skis because the landing of spacecraft requires refined depth perception. Skiing is one sport that develops the ability to judge spatial relationships and slope angles accurately and quickly. In skiing, peripheral vision is also very important so whether in the office, out for a walk or a passenger in a car, spend some time paying particular attention to what you notice at the edges of your vision. Observe too the difference between soft and hard focus. When in soft-focus mode we are more relaxed and receptive to the whole panorama than when focusing intently.

Listening

Your ear is a miraculous organ. It feeds the brain with information that is interpreted into literally thousands of sounds and it can distinguish between the most subtle pitches and tones. With such a marvellous apparatus why is it that we seem to have such difficulty in hearing? Not hearing, not listening, forgetting or even misinterpreting information are common habits. Boredom, distractions and unconscious automatic selection are the cause of this type of deafness.

From now on why not improve your listening ability? By listening for the nuance in tones of voice and pretending that something or somebody is interesting, even when you're bored stiff, can help you to focus. Open your ears to detect the subtleties of sound in a variety of situations. Do all birds sing the same song? Do all cars sound the same? Listen for the alterations in engine noise as your change gear and accelerate. Tune into everyday sounds, even those of your own body as you breathe and move about. Set yourself a goal to listen selectively when in a crowded room, at a party or at work.

We may have no vocabulary for describing the subtle differences in the sounds of skis on snow but this does not mean that our brains cannot distinguish between them. Sounds make up an important part of our sensory image and are particularly useful when we are denied visual input in flat light.

Feeling

Kinaesthesis is the sense by which bodily position, weight, muscle tension, movement and motion are perceived. This process is obviously worth developing in any sporting activity but in a sport like skiing, where the body is continually changing shape and the demands are so varied, it is essential.

Chapter seven is designed to raise your body awareness. By regularly practising the exercises you will develop greater sensitivity, but by paying attention to what you are feeling and where your limbs are in relation to your centre in all sorts of activities you can maintain awareness throughout the day. Postural awareness is a prerequisite of skilful skiing and cannot be learned overnight so start by becoming conscious of your body right now while reading this page. Can you feel any inappropriate tension? Is the way you are holding you body causing strain in some area? Pay attention to the way you sit at work or in the car and to what you notice as you walk or run. If you regularly practice putting your attention into your body when performing familiar movements and when doing the stretching exercises in chapter seven, it will be easier to focus your attention and feel what is happening once you are on skis.

EXPLORING YOUR SENSES WHILE SKIING

To quieten your mind and allow your body to get on with skiing, it helps to focus on something useful. Asking the mind to observe or do something specific makes it less likely to interfere with negative chatter and it will become a friend, a supportive partner. By tuning into your senses your body will receive valuable information and discover what is actually happening, both within and without.

Choose some easy terrain and ask yourself one question at a time to avoid scattering your attention. Ideally all your 'feelers' need to be on the alert, but to start with you may find that, for example, by focusing on seeing, sounds become less obvious. With a lot of practice you will reach a state in which your awareness expands to include everything. I find that listening to my skis helps me to relax and my vision improves.

For all these awareness exercises there is a short, preparation process that is worth doing first. That of clarifying your intention and making a commitment to yourself 'to play the game'. There are bound to be distractions, both external and internal, so be clear that everything else takes second place for the time being. Adding labels, having opinions or judgements about what you see, hear or feel only separates you from experiencing directly.

That's all very well, you might say, but all I can think about is how I'm going to stop, or how I should be doing it! The voice in the head will always interfere if you allow it. *Like anything else, awareness takes practice, so spend some time on a slope that you find really easy.* A slope that poses no threat or increase in heartbeat. If that means walking around on the flat with no slope in sight, then that is where you need to be to begin skiing from the inside.

CHANGING THE NAME OF THE GAME

Until this point the 'game' has been called 'learning to ski', and the mind's conceptual understanding of this is a step-by-step, analytical approach, in which judgements of right and wrong hold sway. The mind can be more usefully employed in the process of learning if we name the game 'developing awareness' rather than 'learning to ski'. If the outer game is too important, it will tend to play you whereas it is the inner game which is the key to everything.

The game is not going to be skiing and a certain set of targets to achieve. *Please let go of what you think you should be doing and any expectations about what will happen*. What you are going to do is explore your senses and develop relaxed concentration. When you become reasonably skilful, you can then take your skill to a slope that will give you some interference to deal with. First, let's have an experience of what it means to have a quiet mind. To be on skis in a state of heightened awareness.

SKIING WITH A QUIET MIND

What was your dominant sense in the exercise we did earlier? Start with that sense since it is the one you are most familiar with. It is important to find out first what *is* happening before you introduce any variation in your focus. So, depending on which sense you choose, ask yourself one of the following questions. If it was not clear which system you prefer, it means that you are an 'alternator' and use all representational systems with equal facility. In this case any of the questions will do.

VISUAL	What am I seeing?
	or
AUDITORY	What am I hearing?
	or
KINAESTHETIC	What am I feeling?

** Be committed to the exercise.

** Let go of all the instructions you usually give yourself.

** Let go of what you expect might happen.

** Choose a target that you will ski towards.

** Choose only one question to ask yourself at a time.

** Do the exercise without trying to change anything.

** Stop and reflect on what you discovered.

** Do this exercise several times.

Once you have discovered your habitual pattern, you can ask yourself if there are other things that you could include in your awareness. Your mind will probably boggle at the thought of including so much – and this is not surprising since it cannot deal with everything because of its sequential thinking style. However, the senses can receive and the brain can process an enormous amount simultaneously so start to open yourself to that possibility and recognize your mind's limiting thoughts. When you have explored one sense, you can open yourself to discovering more about your surroundings with another. Eventually, your awareness will expand to include information from all three.

What to look for

The mountain scenery
The general fall-line of the slope
Undulations and changes in pitch
Variations in the fall-line
Differences in snow texture
Other skiers
Trees, rocks and other obstacles
Where you want to go
Two or three turns ahead
Snow patches rather than ice patches
The path rather than the drop off
Contours and 'line' in the moguls
Shadows on a sunny day
Your shadow on a back-lit slope

Many skiers are in the habit of only looking one turn ahead or even at the tips of their skis. This is rather like watching the bonnet of the car while driving and is about as dangerous. If you are a beginner, you may want to look down at your skis to help you to know where they are and what they are doing. This is useful for a while, but, if you do this, look ahead as well. The sooner you can *feel* what they are doing and look ahead most of the time the better and safer will be your skiing.

Ask yourself, 'Am I really seeing the texture of the snow, the changes in the fall-line and the undulations and irregularities?' When we are relaxed and truly seeing, the eyes flow back and forth, selecting relevant information from far and near. With experience, slope angle, snow speed and other skiers can be taken into account and adjustments made. It is almost as if additional antennae are at work since most of this information is being dealt with unconsciously.

Softening the focus

Sometimes it is as if we can't see for looking. So often when we are anxious or unsure we have tunnel vision, severely inhibiting our ability to deal with what is ahead and magnifying the sensation of going fast. Fear is self-defeating. This narrowing of the vision is a self-imposed limit to the amount of information we allow to filter through for processing into images. The sensation of 'going too fast' is brought about by the reduction in information.

Soften your focus to include the whole landscape and notice how the sensation of speed decreases as you give your body more information about where it is. On discovering this all-inclusive 'soft-focus', many clients tell me that they feel as if they have connected with the mountains for the first time.

What to listen for

The sound of your skis
Differences in snow texture

Differences between left and right turns
Differences between the beginning and ending of turns
Your pole plant
The squeak of your boots
Your clothing as you move
Your breathing
The rush of the wind
Other skiers
Mechanical sounds of piste machines or ski lifts

Are you really hearing everything that is going on around you? Can you notice the sounds that your skis make on different snow textures, from squeaky fresh powder snow to ice? Is one of your skis playing a different tune from the other? Which part of the ski does the sound come from – the front, the middle or the tail?

What to feel

If you are a beginner or are getting back on your skis for the first time after a break, here is a useful exercise to help you to become more aware of these strange appendages. I do this when about to use skis that I am not familiar with, to get a feel for them.

1. Slide your feet back and forth, feeling the smoothness of the soles of the skis against the snow.
2. With your ski poles in the ground for stability, lift one ski up about 15cm (6 in) so it is parallel to the ground. Point your toes to the left and then to the right so that the front of the ski swings like the wiper blades of a car. Feel the swing weight of the ski. Repeat a few times and then change feet.
3. Now imagine that your feet have grown. Your toes are way out there at the tip of the ski and your heels at the tail. Swing the ski as before, feeling the tip and tail as part of your body. Repeat with either foot a couple of times, letting the ski become an extension of your body.

Raising awareness of what you are feeling may take time if you are not naturally tuned into your body. So be patient and begin by asking yourself what you *can* feel. To start with, attend to one thing at a time as you ski. As you become more aware, you may feel many sensations simultaneously:

> Your feet
>
> Pressure points on the soles of your feet
>
> The changing pressure patterns underfoot
>
> The contact of your shins on the front of your boots
>
> Your ankles
>
> The contact of your skis on the snow
>
> The pressure change from one foot to the other
>
> The moment of edge change
>
> The degree of edge as you turn
>
> The inside ski (floating ski)
>
> The inner leg
>
> Your hands and arms
>
> The touch of your pole plant
>
> Your breathing
>
> The flow of your centre into the turn
>
> Your facial expression

Follow your interest

In doing the visual, auditory and kinaesthetic exercises above you may find your attention grasped by something. The texture of the snow, the sound of your skis at the end of the turn or the feeling in your toes at the beginning of a turn. It is important to follow this interest. Not only will it keep you involved in something that is happening *now* but strangely the body does know best and very often it talks to us in its own language. Whenever clients insist on following their interests in a certain direction when I think they could be paying attention to something else, without fail those interests prove to be invaluable for their learning. Remember awareness produces change. Trust your body to tell you what it needs to explore.

HOW TO DEEPEN YOUR AWARENESS

There are no limits to awareness. Only the mind creates limits to what we can experience. In order to deepen your awareness of what is happening all that you need to do is to identify a specific focus, follow a questioning process and remain detached about the feedback that you receive. What we are after is pure observation without judgements of right or wrong, good or bad or analysis of any sort.

The mind habitually comments and wants to chip in, instantly taking us away from the experience of the present moment, so be patient and gently bring your attention back each time you find yourself listening to the mind. Getting annoyed with the mind's interference is only more 'mind stuff' and 'trying to control the mind' is more of the same! Smiling at the mind's monkey tricks and ignoring the voice works wonders.

Remember that the mind knocks at the door and you have the choice to open the door and let it in or not. I thank my mind for calling and politely say, 'Not right now. I'm occupied with something else,' and return to my sensory focus. The mind uses all sorts of disguises to regain control – complications and distractions are favourite ploys. It is really very amusing to observe and if you can keep a light-hearted approach its power will diminish dramatically.

ALLOWING AWARENESS TO PRODUCE CHANGE

There may be something in your body that you would like to be more aware of – some tension or awkwardness, the movement of your upper body, arms or legs. In order to explore whatever it is, the following questioning process is invaluable:

WHAT?   Asking yourself this question will help you
                to identify what you want to focus on.

                'What do I feel?'

WHEN?   Now take it one step further by asking
                yourself, 'When do I feel . . . ?'

WHERE?   Now take it even further by asking
                    yourself, 'Where exactly do I feel . . . ?'

HOW MUCH?   Once you have identified exactly *what*, *when*
                    and *where*, you can rate *how much* on a scale
                    of 1 to 10.

The scenario might go something like this:

> 'I am feeling tense. It is happening all the time but
> particularly at the start of the turn. I am feeling it in my
> upper body. Mostly in my arms and hands. On a scale of
> 1 to 10 it is a 9. Now it is a 7. Now it is a 4. Now it is a 6.
> Now it is a 5. Now it is a 3. Where is it? Nothing in my
> left arm but my right hand is gripping the pole tightly.
> How much on a scale of 1 to 10? A 5. Now it is a 3 . . .'
> and so on.

You will notice that the attention shifted from both arms and
hands to one hand. This shift of focus often happens as the
process evolves. Each time it does just acknowledge that you are
shifting focus, having achieved greater awareness, refocus on the
what, where and when and continue with the rating. If there is
more than one focus, ask yourself which you notice more and
then follow that. You may need to clarify the precise part of the
turn. If you feel stuck, ask yourself what else you are noticing
and what you would like to achieve.

You can adapt this exercise for different senses: 'What do I hear?'
'When do I hear . . .?' and 'How much do I hear . . . ?' For example:

> 'I can hear a loud skidding sound. It happens most at the
> end of my turn. It is coming from the tail of my ski. On a
> scale of 1 to 10 it's an 8 on the right ski and a 5 on the left.
> Now it is a 7 on the right and a 5 on the left,' and so on.

What tends to happen is something that never ceases to amaze
me – the body, given this refined and accurate information,
automatically makes an adjustment that brings greater efficiency
and effortlessness to movement.

Exercises for focused awareness

There are certain activities and areas of the body that benefit
enormously from this sort of focused awareness:

Ankles You may be interested to find out how much your ankles are flexing. By paying attention to the feeling of your shins against the fronts of your boots and rating the degree of pressure 0 to 3 you will give yourself accurate feedback.

Edging Different slope angles, radii of turns and speeds require subtle changes in ski edge angle. It is impossible to say when, where and how much edge tilt is needed and only by raising your awareness of the sensation of grip that you feel through your feet and the differences between grip and glide will your body learn to respond appropriately. Rate the sensation of a flat ski with no grip 0 and rate the varying degrees of edge on a scale 1 to 5. The numbers will vary during the turns, so feel what works. In this way you can focus your attention on the sensations and subtle differences, thus providing your body with the input and feedback it needs to get the feel for what works in different situations.

Pressure How much of your body weight are you committing to the ski as you turn? If your weight is distributed equally on each foot, you will experience 50 per cent of your body weight on each ski. The game here is to feel how much you stand against the turning ski. Is it 70, 80, 90 or 100 per cent? Find out first what is actually happening. It may vary: you may find that you commit more weight to your left ski than your right or vice versa. When you have discovered this, you may like to experiment and play with different percentages. Find out what works.

Distance You may be interested to find out whether you have a stance that assists your balancing. If your feet are very close together, you are unstable and much more likely to fall over. By observing the distance between your feet and calling out the measurement you will raise your awareness of what is happening. Eventually, your body will naturally adopt a stance that feels more balanced. It was doing this exercise that I discovered how awareness could produce change.

Remember to be detached about results while playing these games. Notice if you start 'trying hard to make things happen', manipulating the game to your ends.

After delving this deep into awareness you may need to shift your attention into something more expansive and imaginative for a while.

THE POWER OF THE METAPHOR

Switching hemisphere dominance from left to right and becoming more 'whole brained' cannot be done at will since that forceful, decision-making part of us is largely encompassed by the type of functioning we are wanting to set aside. Instead of a verbal, dominating style the right hemisphere functions as a silent, receptive state of awareness: a conceptual surrendering, a letting go of trying, effort and mental limitations.

This is where the power of metaphor and the imagination can help. By engaging the mind in a game that naturally playful and spontaneous part of us can emerge – children can teach adults a lot about learning! Once again, by changing the name of the game, we release ourselves from mental limitations and create space for the part of us that understands movement patterns, rhythm and spatial relationships to express itself.

There's one game that stands out above all others as a perfect metaphor for skiing, one that is enjoyed by people of all ages. When you play this game, make it your own , not mine, letting it develop to assist your awareness and enjoyment. It is always more fun to share a game so enrol a couple of friends. You will be amazed at how creative and lively people become when they are given an opportunity to play. Choose terrain that you feel comfortable on so that you can let yourself get involved in the game.

The Magical Mystery Tour

The vehicle that we use to take us into the non-verbal, feeling world is a car. Choose any model, the one that you would buy if you could. It can be a sports car, a large comfortable cruiser or a four-wheel drive jeep. So just ask yourself the question 'What is the car of my dreams?' 'What colour is it?' If you have chosen your friendly old banger, that's fine if you feel more comfortable, but you may feel like changing to a different model later on. Or you may have chosen a Formula 1 racing car and find that you feel safer in a saloon car.

When you have decided on the make, model and colour, you

can get into the driver's seat and turn on the engine. Brrrm, brrrm. Making noises will help you to get into the game. You may feel silly to start with; just notice this left-brain chatter trying to interfere and tell it politely that it is a spoil sport. Remember that when you drive a car, you look well ahead and plan your route, giving way to other vehicles. We don't want any dents or scrapes on the bodywork. You may be wondering about the steering wheel. In this car it is low, rather like a bus but not fixed, so don't be tempted to hold your arms stiffly or too high.

To begin with just make the noises. When you are comfortable with that, then check the suspension. This car may be different in certain details from the 'real thing'; its suspension needs to be soft and bouncy to cope with the irregularities in the terrain and cornering. If it stiffens up, imagine squirting oil into your ankles, knees and hips and let all the joints soften up. You don't need to try. Just let the car do the work for you. Brrrm, brrrm!

If you feel that you are driving the car from the back seat, you may want to choose a shallower slope so that you can loosen up and let yourself get into the driving seat. You may notice that the suspension is different while turning, with one leg softer than the other. Explore this relationship, letting the inner leg soften more than the outside turning leg. Overly stiff suspension is common on the outside leg so, if this is the case, spend some time letting it soften, particularly in the ankle.

Once you are comfortable with your suspension, which may take a few runs, you can start to notice if you are using the accelerator pedal appropriately. When driving a real car round a corner, the accelerator pedal is pressed gently through the curve in order to maintain traction. In skiing it is the same except the accelerator pedal needs to be pressed a little earlier. You will find two accelerator pedals between the tongue of the boot and your shin bone on each leg.

Start the engine again – brrrm, brrrm – check the suspension is soft and then focus your attention on your lower shin bones, feeling for the pressure of the accelerator pedal on the turning, outside ski. You may begin to feel as if you are really driving the car rather than being thrown about in the back seat. Experiment with increases in pressure throughout the turn and feel how early you can apply the pressure. Take time exploring these games, allowing your body to assimilate any new feelings. Don't let your mind rush you out of one game and into another or into trying to focus on more than one thing at a time.

Now for the headlights. They are fixed on the knees and shine straight ahead. So choose what colour and intensity they are – white, yellow, orange, green or blue, whatever you fancy. You may find your mind interfering with comments like, 'How can I think about suspension, engine noise, accelerator pedal and headlights all at the same time!' The truth is that you cannot *think* about more than one thing at a time but it is possible for the body to *feel* many things simultaneously. So let go of thinking about anything and simply start off by checking your suspension is soft, that you are in contact with the accelerator pedals and then put your attention into the headlamps on your knees.

You may not be conscious of anything else. That's fine. Just notice where your headlamps are pointing. If you are steering your skis in a plough or a stem the beams may join up. That's perfect for now. As you become more confident and committed to standing against the turning ski, they may naturally shine parallel from time to time. The game is to let your headlamps shine into the next turn, lighting up the way for you. If you feel a lack of control, let the headlamps shine a little further uphill at the end of the turn before starting the new turn. There is an odd connection in this car between the headlights, steering and control – can you find the connection? Check that you are still in touch with the accelerator pedal throughout the turn to assist your steering.

When you have played with the accelerator and headlamps for a few runs, you may be interested to notice what sort of grip your tyres are getting. When driving a car, if you turn the steering wheel too sharply the back end of the car will tend to swing out, especially if the road is slippery. The same is true on skis. We need to set the turn up and let it happen. Let the skis do the turning for us.

What tends to happen when learning to ski is that there is not a great deal of trust that the skis will do the turning so there is a rush at the beginning of the turn to get the feet into the opposite traverse, resulting in a skidded, zig-zag turn. Your car prefers more rounded, smoother arcs and this vehicle has extraordinary tyres that grip on the inside edges. The main difference between your car and a real one is that this car has only two wheels and will only really grip and turn when on one wheel.

So, observe how committed you are to one-wheel turning by feeling how little work the inner leg/wheel is doing throughout the turn. (Some people think that they change pressure to the outside ski completely only to put some weight back on the inside ski once the turn is underway.) To help you focus, re-create your car as vividly as possible and feel the grip of the tyres on the snow. You may notice that the tyres sound different during different parts of the turn. Listen to where the sound is coming from. Move the sound up and down the ski and experiment with making smoother sounds. Just like a car, a severe skid will have more screech.

Keep the game light and fun. Play it for its own sake rather than to achieve certain results. If you are getting intense about things and starting to analyse, criticize or self-instruct, just notice this and let go of your attachment to results. Stay in the process, flow with what *is* happening, not what isn't. Even if what you are doing is not what you think you 'should' be doing.

FINDING RHYTHM

The skier within loves music and appreciates rhythm. You could turn on the music in your car to blow the cobwebs away, and sing to yourself as you ski. Even if you don't have much of a voice, the memory of a tune will spark off something in your body. My favourites are 'I could have danced all night', 'Take it easy' and 'Summertime'. It doesn't seem to matter that I don't know all the words; by simply switching my attention to a song the internal chatter ceases. Choose a song that suits the tempo of the terrain and let the tempo of the song change if it needs to, to fit in with your skiing. No one is listening – most people are too concerned about themselves to be bothered with whether you are in tune!

Sometimes when I'm singing I notice something about my skiing that leads me into another awareness game. My interest gets sparked by a feeling and the mind becomes quiet and my attention is focused once more.

Listening to music

You may have a personal stereo that you could take with you skiing. A word of warning here: **In order not to be a danger to**

yourself or to others, keep the volume level low so that you can hear other people, piste machines and voices around you. Many people find that listening to music solves many of their skiing 'problems'. They discover rhythm and their minds are quietened by the music. Personally, I do not like listening to music while skiing since I enjoy hearing the subtle sounds of the snow and my skis. What works for me is to listen to music while riding the lift and enjoying the scenery and then turning it off before starting to ski. The tune and rhythm stay with me and I can hear the sounds that my skis make – the best of both worlds!

Now!

If you want to develop more rhythm in your skiing, first check that you are using your ski poles as described in chapter three. A game that helps to focus the mind and provide you with useful feedback it to say 'now' at the exact moment that you *feel* your ski pole touch the snow. Say the word out loud so that you can hear the rhythm of your turns. When you have done this for a little while, ask yourself the question, 'Am I accurate?' Check that you are saying the word *exactly* as you feel the pole touch the snow, not before or after. I find this game particularly helpful in the moguls or whenever I need more commitment in my skiing.

Counting

Another way of developing rhythm is to count during your ski turns. One, two, three. One, two, three. This is very helpful if you are finding that you are rushing through the fall-line and making zig-zag turns instead of smooth, rounded arcs. You may find that you can count to five instead of to three. Count out loud and notice the tone of your voice. It may get louder and more tense as you face the fall-line. Experiment by softening the tone for a few turns and then sounding determined and calm.

Exaggerations

A great way to raise awareness is to play the exaggeration game. If you are feeling stiff, pretend you are even stiffer than you are: ski like a soldier marching or a rusty mechanical doll. Then act out the opposite: become a floppy rag doll.

You may have a habit that you would like to change but are not fully aware of. The exaggeration game can help bring the inefficiency into your awareness, and the opposite, exaggerated movement will give your body a chance to break out of the familiar pattern and feel something different.

Harmonizing with the way you feel

It is extraordinary but when we harmonize with the way we feel it often creates the possibility for change. So if you feel jerky or uninspired, go and have a really jerky or uninspired run. If you get totally involved, paradoxically your commitment to the game will provide the energy for transformation. When you ask yourself how you feel, make sure that your reply is a descriptive adjective and not just a judgement like 'good', 'bad' or 'terrible'.

BREATHING

Just as a car will not run smoothly without a well-regulated distributor to give a constant supply of fuel, so the human body and mind will not function smoothly without a regular pattern of breathing to supply adequate oxygen. There is a direct connection between optimum performance and breathing. If there is any holding of the breath or unevenness you can be sure that it is reflected within the body in some way.

So many of my clients admit to holding their breath – not just now and again but sometimes from the top of a slope to the bottom. Needless to say they arrive feeling weak and tense and wondering why they are off-balance. Certainly from my own experience, a catch in my breath is the first signal that all is not well.

This is the single, most effective awareness exercise for bringing body and mind into harmony. Begin noticing your breathing as you ski. Do not change anything or try to force it to take a certain pattern. The first step is to find out what *is* happening simply by attending to the inhale and exhale. In this way your awareness alone will produce an appropriate change. Learn to be an observer. Watch whoever it is within you, breathing you. You may notice that your breathing can take on many different qualities and rhythms to meet the needs of your body. Ideally your lungs fill and empty completely, making your rib cage expand and the chest lift. While skiing, notice if your breathing fits the rhythm of your turns. You may find a rhythm that is helpful in coordinating all your movements.

Because of its importance, breathing is referred to several times in this book. If you practise the stretching exercises in chapter seven, you will begin to learn how breathing and balanced movement are indivisible. Certainly, some of my most memorable moments on skis, when most in harmony with the mountain, have been when my breathing seemed to be doing the skiing for me.

PLAYING THE GAME

There is literally no limit to the variety of games that we can invent to give our minds something useful to do – use your imagination. Once you understand the principle of observing the mind's interference and choosing to return your focus to the game, you will be taking charge of your potential to learn and develop and you will begin to discover that many of the answers to skiing lie inside yourself. In fact, we have such a huge, untapped potential that scientists are continually reducing the estimated amount that we use our brains as they discover more and more about the possibilities and power within.

Chapter Six

The power within

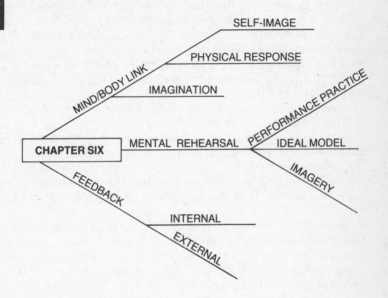

SELF-IMAGE
PHYSICAL RESPONSE
MIND/BODY LINK
IMAGINATION
PERFORMANCE PRACTICE
CHAPTER SIX
MENTAL REHEARSAL
IDEAL MODEL
IMAGERY
FEEDBACK
INTERNAL
EXTERNAL

Fairy tales of frogs turning into princes may sound far-fetched in a skiing context but they're more relevant than you think. The nervous system cannot always tell the difference between a vividly imagined experience and the real thing – it acts on whatever information it is supplied by the mind – so, if you see yourself as being uncoordinated and have thoughts of failure, it is likely that this will be a self-fulfilling prophecy.

Many everyday experiences demonstrate the power of our imagination graphically. Everyone knows what imaginary food can do to their salivary glands. Don't just take this as a statement of fact. If you are in any doubt, try it! What is your favourite food? See it in front of you. What colour or shape is it? Smell it, taste it, notice its temperature and feel its texture in your mouth. You might even convince yourself that you are hungry!

If you are determined to disprove this statement you will of course be able to do so. However, you are still demonstrating the power of your mind. By recognizing this innate power and realizing that every thought causes an internal experience with attendant feelings, you will begin to understand that you can take complete responsibility for your experience on skis.

Many people think that the opposite is true. That the evidence creates the story and that external events are the cause rather than the effect. The mind is very complicated and has been conditioned since childhood to believe certain things and to perform in certain ways. It tends to repeat things over and over, believe them and then project these beliefs externally. We tend to forget that when we 'see' something we are viewing the image as it appears inside our heads and not 'out there' as it really is.

You are seeing these words through your eyes. Your eyes are just receivers that send input from a mass of light waves to the brain to form an internal image of the external world. The awareness that sees, that witnesses, simply observes what is out there. Your mind then names various objects based on stored data and associated past experiences, has opinions and makes judgements.

So we view the world through our personalized, conditioned perspective which may or may not be the whole truth. We project our personal interpretation onto what is out there. We think that the ice patch or the bump is the cause of our falling over, when in fact it is our mind's internal workings which create the fall. The fear, the tension and the stiffening all happen within us while the ice patch minds its own business. The ice patch has no power over us. The truth is that, once we have a reasonable amount of experience, nothing is responsible for making us fall except our minds. Obviously it is more difficult to ski on ice and someone with less feeling for balancing on skis will have less chance of coping. Someone who has never skied is likely to fall frequently in all sorts of situations as he or she explores a new world. However, a relaxed attitude can minimize this.

To show you how powerfully your imagination is linked with your nervous system and automatic physical response, imagine you are at Wimbledon. You are up in the stands to the side of the Centre Court, looking down at the match in progress. The grass is green and the lines of the court are clearly marked out. The server is on your right and you see the ball leave his hand, hear it make contact with his racket and travel over the net to be returned by the other player.

Having read this far, close your eyes, lightly place your hands over your eyeballs and re-create the scenario above.

Now re-create the same scene but from the point of view of the ball boy crouched down by the net. You may have felt your eyeballs and/or head respond to your internal images in the first example, and this is likely to be even more pronounced from a different point of view. The point is that your body responds consciously or unconsciously to every image that you create.

If you believe that you are the victim of every ice patch on the mountain, that projection will create for you a myriad of situations which will provide evidence that ice patches *are* out to get you. Just recognizing that you are responsible for your experience will create a fundamental shift in the beliefs you hold and thus a major change in your response to external events. To master skiing you need to enrol your mind and direct it towards a more constructive contribution that will enhance your performance.

YOU MAY NOT BE WHO YOU THINK YOU ARE

When I was a freestyle competitor, falling over in the ballet event was a fairly regular occurrence – and I could always find plenty of excuses or reasons for losing balance. At one competition there had been a recent fall of snow and the conditions were causing the best in the world to stumble and fall. I completed my run without a hitch, much to everyone's surprise, including mine. On reflection, I realized that 'heavy snow' was a skiing condition that had never bothered me and the underlying programme which controlled me that day was 'I like heavy snow; it is a challenge'. This programme had overridden the concerns that usually scattered my attention.

We have many of these underlying programmes and they vary from role to role and situation to situation. All together they make up our self-image – the way we see ourselves – and it is this which influences our degree of success in any activity. This self-image is something that we have created from the moment we were able to have thoughts, compare ourselves with others and form opinions about ourselves. Some of the opinions we have adopted were originally somebody else's judgement about us, some are based on the way we would like to see ourselves and some are direct looking-glass reflections.

Your self-image is the person you think you are, who you imagine yourself to be, a composite of remembered past experiences and their outcomes. This differs from role to role and can change from day to day, depending on your expectations and your physical and mental fitness. The mind makes continual modifications, based on prevailing evidence and new interpretations of past experiences.

I shall never forget the woman who described herself as 'completely uncoordinated' and volunteered for a ball throwing and catching exercise at an Inner Tennis Course years ago. She approached the front of the group with her arms held stiffly by her sides. As the ball approached her, she recoiled, her arms lifting uselessly after the ball had passed. 'You see, I am hopeless,' she said.

She was asked not to try to catch the ball as it approached but just to watch it and answer questions about it. It was obvious to us that she did not see the ball when it was getting close. Gradually, since the game was not to catch the ball but just to observe it, and there was fundamentally nothing wrong with her eyesight, the questions allowed her awareness to deepen and she began to watch the ball, not as a threat but as an interesting round object travelling towards her at different heights, with varying rotations and characteristics. Then, hesitantly, her hands began seeking the ball, at first tentatively and then with greater confidence and regularity.

The group could not contain itself and the exclamations drew her attention to what was happening. For an instant her mind rejected the truth that she was not after all 'hopelessly uncoordinated' and her body regained its initial stiffness. A little grin widened into a huge beaming smile as she recognized her mental programme and let it go in favour of the new-found awareness of the ball in her hands.

I was intrigued and amazed by this transformation. Apparently an early experience in school, where she was judged harshly and made to feel foolish in front of her peers, had started this self-image of zero coordination and hopelessness. 'My reaction at the moment is of anger,' she commented, 'that I wasted so much of my adult life avoiding all ball games, but I am thrilled to have discovered I am not who I thought I was and perhaps I can become a tennis player after all.'

The truth about the self-image is that it is usually inaccurate and often incomplete. It also tends to get stuck in a self-perpetuating mould. Since it influences the outcome of any action, an unconstructive self-image will tend to produce the evidence to perpetuate itself.

Our culture and education system support this self-destruction by harping on the negative rather than the positive, the 'what you did wrong' rather than the 'what you did right'. Many of us have the habit of recalling only the two ski turns that were awkward rather than the ten that flowed, and many people's minds are so conditioned by negative self-images that they are completely lost without feedback of what they did wrong.

There are certain characteristics that betray a destructive self-image, and you may find it interesting to observe them in others or yourself. In the extreme, the body will hold itself in a defensive or dejected pose with a scowl or frown. There is likely to be little motivation to do anything, little ambition or enthusiasm. Moaning and criticizing themselves and others, they even tear down other people's hopes and dreams of success and their favourite word is 'can't'.

You may not recognize yourself at all in the above description and have a nourishing, positive attitude to yourself as a skier or perhaps there are facets of your self-image that do not empower you. If, like most people, you do recognize moments when you indulge in self-criticism of lack of trust, begin to notice every time you make a negative judgement which bolsters a poor self-image. Make a note of what the voice says so that you can get to know how you sabotage your potential. Notice how critical and unforgiving you are, dwelling on the less effective aspects of your performance.

A fall is only evidence that something did not work. It does not have to be an opportunity to beat yourself up. Feelings of awkwardness and errors are valuable feedback and require our attention within the context of our whole performance but there is no value in rating them in terms of 'good' or 'bad'. The moment we judge, we lose the chance of learning the truth about what happened.

Perhaps somewhere in the past there was an experience that resulted in a decision or opinion about your ability. The truth of the moment might have been that a lack of muscular strength or concentration, inappropriate technique or selection of terrain contributed to an ineffective performance. Or perhaps at some time someone gave you feedback that what you were doing was 'wrong', or that you 'never plant your pole'. A lack of initial success does not need to colour all future attempts and get stuck as a negative pattern.

These beliefs or programmes acquired consciously or unconsciously since birth will influence every action we make. *What you see and feel about yourself is what you get*. If you have a vision of falling every time your other half watches you ski, then it is highly likely that you will. Similarly if you have a voice telling you that it is too late to learn, progress is unlikely however many lessons you take. Having a negative 'I always . . .' programme means you are repeatedly preparing yourself for failure and limiting the expression of your potential. The is probably why the use of so-called 'positive thinking' or 'will power' is ineffectual when the underlying attitudes are contradictory.

Now for the good news; since it was 'you' that created your poor self-image in the first place, you can become conscious of it, recognize its invalidity and begin to let it go and replace the negative thoughts and images with more positive ones. There is now a great deal of evidence to support our ability to change these underlying programmes by imagining a different behaviour pattern and repeating an affirmation to the subconscious, so reprogramming our internal computers. So whatever your self-image, it is possible to improve and build on the fundamentals which can affect your performance without even putting on a pair of skis.

You may feel some resistance to letting go of part of your self-image. A habit is familiar, even though it might have no benefit! It feels comfortable, like those old clothes that you won't part with. The resistance may take the form of lethargy or 'Well, I've always been a negative person. A leopard can't change its spots.' Inertia will hold us back if we let it and only consciously directed energy, or awareness, can effect change. Just notice any resistance and rate your current level of commitment to improving your skiing on a scale of 1 to 10.

Self-image exercise

So halt awhile and examine your own story. How do you see yourself in the context of skiing? Rate on a scale of 1 to 10 your answers to the following questions (1 = not at all and 10 = yes). Write down the first number that comes to mind. This is only intended to assist your enquiry, so be as honest as you can!

1. Do I always describe my skiing in a positive way?
2. Am I confident about my ability to cope with a challenge?
3. Do I believe it is possible to become a proficient skier given my age? . . . sex? . . . fitness?
4. Do I believe I am reasonably coordinated?
5. Do I rarely have anxious thoughts?
6. Do I trust my body to take care of balancing?
7. Is my skiing progressing?
8. Am I unconcerned about spectators when I ski under a lift? .
9. When I fall, do I view it as an opportunity to learn something?
10. Do I have fun and enjoy skiing?
11. Do I find it easy to relax in tricky conditions?
12. Do I infrequently chastise myself, encouraging myself with supportive self-talk instead?

The higher the score the more your self-image empowers you. You may find that you have a low score and recognize mental habits that are inhibiting your progress. That's fine. Recognition of these habits is already half way to changing them. No matter what you have discovered, you can revamp your self-image and develop your ability to visualize so that your mind can work for you rather than against you. If your self-image is already productive, then the exercises will help you to progress even faster.

To take charge of re-creating a more productive self-image, we must first get to know our defeatist tendencies. Then, once recognizing the trigger or situation that sets the pattern off, we can repattern our response with something more supportive. Our unhelpful 'stories' have been repeated over and over, so in order to redress the balance some repetitive affirmation may be necessary.

AFFIRMATIONS

They can because they think they can

Virgil

An affirmation is a short powerful statement to yourself that feeds the subconscious with qualities that are more productive. If you find some resistance to doing the following exercise, you can be sure that it will be valuable and is worth persevering.

Have a notebook and pen handy, make sure you are sitting comfortably with your arms and legs uncrossed, you spine erect and supported. Refer to the self-image questionnaire above. For example, if you had a low score on questions 2, 8 or 11, you could adopt the following affirmation:

'I . . . (your name) am relaxed, alert and centred over my skis. Everything comes to me easily and effortlessly. I remain calm and focused even when presented with distractions or a challenge.'

Or if you had low scores on questions 4 or 6 you could adopt the following:

'I . . . (your name) am relaxed, alert and centred over my skis. I trust my body to coordinate smooth, flowing movements and remain balanced.'

It is of course more effective to make up your own affirmation, using the words that mean most to you. So spend a little time on this. *The secret is to repeat the affirmation in the present tense as if it were true, even if you don't believe it – yet.* How would it *feel* to be the way your affirmation suggests? You can get into the habit of repeating your affirmation to yourself at odd times during the day and before you go to sleep at night.

Regular, short practices from now until you go skiing will groove in a new attitude and pattern of thought. You may not believe in your affirmation at the beginning and have contradictory thoughts. Just notice those thoughts, smile at their persistence and view them as past history. Let them go, refocusing on the new feelings and thoughts. Trust your subconscious to deal with the rest. Turning frogs into princes may not be so crazy after all!

MENTAL REHEARSAL

Over the past few years mental rehearsal, or visualization as it is commonly known, has been accepted by many athletes as a powerful means of clarifying patterns of movement and rehearsing a performance. The word 'visualize' is a misnomer because it suggests that the mental image is exclusively visual when in practice the other senses become involved. However, it is in common (mis)usage.

We humans are goal-seeking 'machines' that steer a path to a target by use of pre-programmed data, sensory input and feedback. Each time you vividly imagine yourself performing an action, the neural pathways in the brain spark in response and minute muscle movements result. Obviously, we all inherit slightly different bodies with strengths and weaknesses that develop into tendencies, characteristics and our unique personalities – so imagining you are Klammer or Stenmark may not perform an immediate miracle. However, by focusing on their qualities and patterns of movement, you are suggesting an ideal to your brain and at a subliminal level some elements will be assimilated, helping you to express different qualities.

Visualization was an unknown technique when I started skiing. 'Daydreaming' was the term I might have used for those moments when I would imagine myself skiing my favourite slope. During the summer months, longing for winter to come around again, I would dream of how it was going to be when I ventured into fresh powder snow for the first time. The images were of experts that I had watched the previous winter and a ski film that had impressed me. I would recall their movements, rhythm and lightness and imagine myself making my own tracks behind them.

When winter did eventually come round and an opportunity to live out my dreams presented itself, I ventured into the fresh snow at the side of the piste. Turn, turn, crash. Turn, turn, turn, crash. Turn, turn, turn . . . yippee! Later on I realized that I had powerfully programmed myself for success in what I had thought were idle daydreams.

Visualization during the summer months keeps the neural pathways clear of weeds so that you can start closer to where you left off last time. Practised for a few weeks prior to your ski holiday, you can alert your brain to what is in store. Mental rehearsal prior to setting off down a slope can powerfully influence your performance, and reviewing the day's skiing will help consolidate your learning and raise your awareness of areas of unclarity.

We are going to look at six ways of practising mental rehearsal:

PERFORMANCE PRACTICE

IDEAL MODEL

PREPLAY

INSTANT REPLAY

SKIING 'AS IF'

IMAGERY

HOW TO VISUALIZE

Before going into the detail of how to practise the different forms of mental rehearsal, you will need to know something about the technique of visualization. To visualize you need to be both relaxed and alert. The effects of mental rehearsal are very subtle so if your body is tense or uncomfortable that information will be assimilated along with the images and may not be useful. To maintain the quality of your concentration, do the exercises for only two or three minutes at first. When you become more practised and your concentration improves, you can lengthen the time to five or even ten minutes. It is important that you enjoy the process. After all, it is free skiing and there are no risks attached! If you are bored or distracted, it may have a negative effect on your subsequent performance. Lying down tends to encourage sleep rather than an alert mental state. So sit on a chair with your feet on the floor, your spine supported and your arms and legs uncrossed.

For visualization to be most effective you need to be able to re-create as many sensory images as you can – feelings, images of movements and sounds to build a multi-dimensional movie. In skiing, kinaesthetic awareness is the most important but this may not be your preferred sense so you will need to start by re-creating images through the sense that you found easiest to access, whether visual or auditory. When you did the sensory exercise in chapter five, which was your preferred sense? You can build on that by recalling simple kinaesthetic memories, like what clothes you are wearing as you ski and how do they feel?

You may find that at first you are unable to 'be inside' your body and can only view it from the outside. Being outside is useful too, so view yourself from all angles. To get inside your body, pay attention to your hands as you watch yourself; feel them holding the ski poles. You may find that this pulls you into feeling the image and before you know it you will be *skiing from the inside*.

To make the image as alive and vibrant as possible, keep it in the present. Ask yourself questions like 'What am I wearing?' rather than 'What was I wearing?' Keep the sensory movie running at normal speed, unless you wish to explore a particular sequence. In which case, you can slow the movie down to highlight what is happening. Be sure to come back to normal speed again before you finish.

If you have not done a lot of skiing, you may find that you have few sensory images to call upon. This is quite normal and just indicates the current level of your awareness. By doing the awareness exercises in chapter five, you will be supplying your body with the necessary feedback to create images for the future. Even experienced skiers find that there are fuzzy images or gaps in their vizualisation. *These are valuable pointers to lack of awareness in movement patterns and clues as to where the attention needs to be focused while skiing.* Often the body is confused because the movement is being done differently each time or there is an inefficient or awkward habit that needs to be sorted out.

I found this particularly true when I was performing somersaults as a freestyle competitor. Lying in bed at night, the images of the inrun, take off and start of the movement were very clear and yet the ending was a blank. Not a comfortable feeling at all! I realized there was a lack of clarity about landing on snow and skiing away. I had done dozens of training jumps into water but at that time was not experienced on snow. By closely watching other aerialists landing and by raising my awareness of what was happening during my jump, I could complete the imagery of the whole movement, feel my skis make contact with the snow and ski away. My performance improved as well as my sleep.

Regular short-duration practice is more useful than a longer session once a week. When you have got the hang of it, you will be able to switch to your internal movie whenever you like but to start with make sure that you are quiet and free from distractions. You will find it refreshing as a break from mundane chores or at idle moments when sitting on a train or at the hairdressers.

PERFORMANCE PRACTICE

Start by focusing on your breathing and by counting backwards as you inhale and exhale. As your breathing deepens you will be able to count 5.4.3.2.1. on each exhale and inhale. With your eyes closed, do the tension-release exercise from the head down as described in chapter four. When you feel relaxed, re-create the surroundings of your favourite ski resort. See the mountains, the trees and the overall lie of the land. What can you see? Buildings, ski lifts, people? What colours predominate? The whiteness of the snow, the darkness of the rocks on the mountains and the dark green of the trees? Re-create the scene as vividly as you can in your mind's eye.

See yourself carrying your equipment towards the lift. What are you wearing? What colour and texture are your clothes? Does the fabric rustle as you move? Feel your feet firmly supported in your ski boots. What sound do they make as you walk across the snow? How do your skis feel over your shoulder and your poles in your hand?

Now see yourself standing on flat ground at the top of the lift. Look around you and re-create as much of the surroundings as you can – the sounds, sights and even smells. Breathe the fresh clean air and feel the sun on your face. Are you smiling at the prospect of skiing your favourite slope? The one that poses no threat, no problems.

Go through the process of putting on your skis and getting ready to set off. Feel the skis on your feet, slide your skis back and forth and feel the texture of the snow. Look down the slope and see the terrain that you want to ski. When you feel ready, start skiing, and re-create the sensations of sliding and turning. What sounds can you hear? Your skis on the snow, the touch of your pole plant, the wind passing your ears? What can you see ahead of you? Can you see the fall-line of the slope? Can you feel the flow of your centre of mass from one turn to the next? Tune into the rhythm of your turns.

Allow yourself to feel the whole movement of your body as you ski. If you make an awkward turn or fall over, just edit that section by replaying the movie, cutting out the imbalance and re-skiing the turn. Notice your breathing, the rhythm of the turns. You can always come to a stop after a few turns, refocus and start off again. When you have done enough or if your attention starts to wander, come to a stop. Re-create the place where you are practising this mental rehearsal in your mind, wriggle your toes and fingers and open your eyes.

You may have noticed something during the exercise that is worth jotting down in your notebook so that you can check it out when you are next on the slopes.

IDEAL MODEL

It is not surprising that many people find their tennis has improved after watching Wimbledon. Watching ideal images in the comfort of your sitting room may seem the lazy man's way to better performance but when this is done consciously it can be very effective.

Having a stock of images of your favourite skier to call on is a powerful way to influence your skiing. I have vivid images of two skiers that regularly accompany me down the slopes even though they may be miles away. Christina Hornberg from Sweden, an excellent skier who over the years has inspired me with her strong, flowing style and sense of fun: just to recall her skiing lifts my spirits and, perhaps because I am of a similar build, my body connects strongly with the way she moves and expresses herself. The other skier, John Falkiner, although he has a very different body shape to mine, demonstrates a wonderful balance of power and grace. Whenever I need inspiration, I just ask myself, 'How would Christina or John ski this?'

Chinese whispers

A word of warning here about the quality of the images that you copy. I remember training in a group to be a ski instructor; we would watch the trainer do a demonstration and then ski down one at a time. The first skier would get the closest approximation to the demonstration and like Chinese whispers it would become more and more different as each person watched the previous version and unconsciously picked up variations in timing and tempo. My strategy was to watch the trainer demonstrate and then sing to myself and admire the view. When my turn came, I would replay the stored image in my mind before setting off and do my version without too much distortion.

So, if you find yourself in a similar situation at ski school, follow my strategy and give yourself a sporting chance of emulating the instructor's demonstration. If while riding the lifts you tend to watch the people having problems or the flashiest poseur, you are feeding yourself with images that aren't useful. Watch the most efficient, calm, relaxed skiers instead.

Watching other people and copying is one of the most effective ways of learning. Doing this consciously and practising mentally prior to having a go gives the brain a greater chance of success. Reviewing what you felt afterwards in your mind helps your brain to clarify and groove the neural pathways, the pattern of the movement.

You can adapt the earlier visualization exercise to include skiing behind your ideal model. When you are at the top of the slope in your mind's eye, see your ideal ski into frame, say hello and ask you to follow. Watch him or her ski down the slope, looking at the whole body shape, and follow behind. As you follow the rhythm and flow, allow yourself to get inside that body. How would it feel to ski like the ideal? How would it sound? What would you notice? Refer to the next section, on 'shadowing', for more detailed guidelines on how to follow.

On my ski courses, I have taken the ideal model technique one step further, by preparing a special image-replay video of repeated skiing movements accompanied by baroque music. The music helps the brain create alpha waves, a more receptive, relaxed, suggestible state, so the images can be absorbed effortlessly. We watch the video in the comfort of the sitting room and then go skiing with audio cassette players, using the same baroque music to help trigger the images that were absorbed earlier. The differences in performance are often startling.

Sadly the medium of the book does not allow you to share this experience, so all I can recommend is that you watch as many ski films as possible to stock your internal movie library with footage of skiers that appeal to you. Absorb whole patterns of movement and replay them internally at idle moments, while waiting in line at the supermarket or while travelling on public transport. People will wonder at the smile on your face and you will be surprised at the improvement you can make without a snowflake in sight.

Shadowing

Following a more expert skier combines the image with the activity. When following someone, don't just look at the tails of the skis and where their tracks have gone in the snow. Watch the whole body moving in front of you, noticing in particular the flow of the skier's centre and the rhythm of the pole plant. In this way you can really shadow the shape and give your body a feast of input. Imagine you are connected by an invisible umbilical cord and surrender yourself to your leader's route finding. The more you can keep your mind out of the way the better. So focus on your breathing and what you are feeling in response to the visual image in front of you. Once you have discovered new sensations, your body will recognize these feelings of flow and you will be able to repeat them with greater and greater consistency.

PREPLAY

This is a short mental rehearsal done on the slope before you set off. After looking at the terrain ahead, close your eyes for a moment and see the way that you would like to perform. What rhythm of turns, what speed fits the slope, what quality would you like to express? Or perhaps you would like to focus on an aspect of your skiing – your pole plant for instance. See yourself skiing in your mind's eye before you set off. This visual image speaks directly to the body in a way that repeated instructions cannot.

I find this particularly useful in the moguls, where there is a visible pattern of turns to be made. After examining the contours of the slope, I imagine myself skiing a line and adding a quality such as smoothness, lightness or commitment. Or I simply ask myself the question 'How would I ski this if it was easy?'

INSTANT REPLAY

It may be easier to recall sensations immediately after you have experienced them, and this intensity can then be re-created more easily when doing mental rehearsal later on. After skiing some turns, take a few moments to review what you just experienced. This doesn't take long and is very worthwhile. Let go of any judgements of good or bad and just notice what felt effective or inefficient in your movements. Your body will want to repeat movements that felt pleasant, but when changing habits, a new movement may feel 'different' and not as comfortable as the old habit. Examine what works – what produces the results that you are after.

Video feedback

External knowledge of results provides important feedback so if you can see yourself on video it will help your overall awareness. Some people really dislike this form of feedback, possibly because it cuts through illusion and tells the truth! It is useful for helping you create a more accurate visual image of the way you ski. People are often surprised by what they see, 'I thought I was really flexing but now I realize I could get lower'. However, it is only useful when accompanied by a supportive, positive and factual commentary. Many instructors do not fully realize the effect of their criticism and how damaging their overly negative comments can be. Unless you can be sure that your instructor or coach is using video feedback in a supportive and sensitive way, I would not recommend it. If you are doing this amongst friends I suggest the following procedure.

1. View the video first without making any comments at all about yourself or each other. Refrain, if you can, from focusing on what you are doing 'wrong' and judging yourself. Just watch yourself without internal commentary.
2. On second viewing, notice three things that you are doing effectively and that you can acknowledge in your skiing – the colour of your ski suit will not do! Jot them down in your notebook as an affirmation.
3. On third viewing, notice three things that you could do differently or more efficiently. Write these in your notebook so you don't forget. You could work these into a visualization or affirmation for greater effect.

Some people have nothing constructive to say about their skiing and find it hard to appreciate anything about their ability. Be supportive of each other's performance, help each other to recognize what *is* working before you start on what *isn't* and get into the habit of using the words 'effective', 'efficient' and 'ineffective' and 'inefficient' without value judgements attached.

SKIING 'AS IF'

This technique is practised when you are not on the slopes and lets your imagination have full rein. Allow yourself to become relaxed by focusing on your breathing. Follow each breath in and out while counting backwards from 5. Inhale 5.4.3.2.1; exhale 5.4.3.2.1. If you feel tense or your attention is scattered, do the tension-release exercise in chapter four first. When you feel relaxed and focused on your breathing, repeat the affirmation that you made earlier on two or three times. Then do the following exercise:

1. Recall your most successful descent on skis. This may be three linked turns on a nursery slope or a run in steep moguls.
2. Rerun it a couple of times in your imagination with your eyes closed.
3. Re-create as much detail as possible, e.g. what you were wearing, feelings, sounds, sights, the sunshine, the snow and the smile on your face.

4. Recall the affirmation you created earlier on. Adopt each new quality in turn 'as if' it were part of your skiing. How would it look? Dare to become . . . How would it feel?
5. Repeat to yourself this affirmation. 'This . . . (new quality) is part of my skiing. As I focus on this . . . (new quality), it becomes part of me. Everything comes to me easily and effortlessly. *Everything I need is already within me.*'

Regular short practices can enhance your performance, adding to your confidence and smoothing out your movements. Adopt the habit of visualizing yourself skiing and realize what an enjoyable, safe and cheap means of increasing your mileage it is.

Heavy or light?

There are times when our movements feel heavy and slow – a vast contrast to those moments when we feel light and invincible. By exaggerating and acting out the two extremes of the spectrum it is possible to change our experience. This was never more apparent than with one client, who would fall and not be able to get up – even with help! It was as if she was stuck to the ground. She was not particularly overweight so I was perplexed by my inability to help her up.

After a couple of exhausting days for both of us, I asked her if she *actually wanted* to get up. 'Well, now you mention it, no, I don't. I feel safer down here.' Later I did some tests with a friend while thinking 'heavy' and thinking 'light'. It was extraordinary – we could dramatically influence the difficulty or ease with which we could lift each other off the ground. We had solved the riddle. Unconsciously the client was thinking herself into the ground, thinking 'heavy'. So how would it be if you skied as if you were twenty pounds lighter?

IMAGERY

This is another, different use of the imagination. In this technique we borrow the qualities that we associate with an object and bring them into our skiing. It is a very personal process. What means something to me, may not necessarily mean the same thing to you. So it is always best to create your own image rather than borrow someone else's – unless of course it appeals to you. I have found over the years that there are certain images that most people plug into with ease, especially when they have added their own personal details. For example, the overall image in 'The Magical Mystery Tour' (see chapter five) is a car but the colour, make and model are your choice.

Using imagery can add different qualities to your skiing at a stroke. When first asked to ski 'like a bird', my reaction was one of disgust since it implied wafting aimlessly in the sky, and 'wafting' and 'aimlessness' were not qualities that I wanted to add to my skiing. I resisted vehemently, but fortunately my coach was persistent and cajoled me into having a go. What an extraordinary discovery I made! By choosing a bird that knew where it wanted to go and by skiing softer rather than harder, my turns began to develop a power and control out of all proportion to the effort I was applying. 'Birds' has since been one of my favourite games, adding lightness, grace and power when I get bogged down in 'trying hard'.

Here are some qualities that you might like to experiment with. Be honest – what does your skiing lack?

> Grace
>
> Fluidity/flow
>
> Flexibility
>
> Smoothness
>
> Control
>
> Confidence
>
> Effortlessness
>
> Power
>
> Versatility

Think of something which represents the quality you are after: a willow, a lion, a bird, a four-wheel drive vehicle? Spend a few moments really seeing that image in your mind. Create its colour, shape, movement. Then just hold the image in your mind as you ski, allowing your body to become the image and express as much of the quality as you can. Choosing an appropriate image for the terrain that you are on is important. Skiing like a mouse in the moguls may not be effective, unless it is a hungry mouse, the cheese is at the bottom of the slope and it is being chased by an even hungrier cat!

One client had me in stitches one day as he skied as if he was John Cleese – he wanted more variety, versatility and fun, so the sketch of 'The Ministry of Funny Walks' was ideal. That may be an extreme case but it suited his mood at that moment perfectly. He began to relax and truly express his potential.

Here are some ideas to help you choose an image:

GRACE	Bird, dancer, panther, swan
FLUIDITY/FLOW	River, cascade of water, willow in the wind
FLEXIBILITY	Gorilla, rubber legs, springs
SMOOTHNESS	Silk, marshmallow legs, chocolate sauce pouring over ice-cream moguls
CONTROL	Four-wheel drive vehicle, dressage horse
CONFIDENCE	Lion, hawk, warrior
EFFORTLESSNESS	Bird, impala, cheetah
POWER	Warrior, boxer, bouncer

Experiment with different images. Some will seem to suit better than others. Use your imagination – the image must mean something to you. One of my favourites is a larch tree: roots firmly planted in the earth, strong trunk, graceful branches and able to withstand all sorts of stormy weather by being strong, yet flexible.

You may be thinking, 'How bizarre! She's stark raving mad.' Perhaps, and your judgement might mean that you miss out on a quantum leap in your skiing. If you only give a half-hearted stab at imagery, you will only, if you are lucky, get half the possible results. If you feel bashful about skiing like a bird, don't tell anyone. It'll be our secret. There are already hundreds of birds disguised as skiers on the piste. When the image starts to work for you, you'll be crowing all over the mountain.

Chapter Seven

Tuning the vehicle

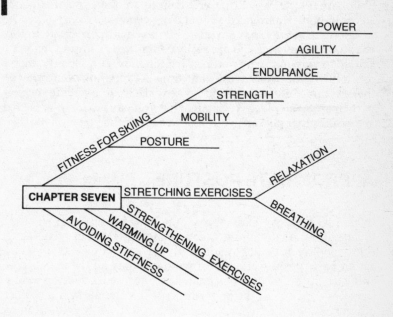

THE CARROT

Hopefully you won't skip this chapter. After all, if you want your car to run smoothly, you have it serviced, tuned and then keep it topped up with oil. If you don't look after it, drive it hard and carelessly, then it is very likely to conk out. Certainly this is true of skiers. It is extraordinary how many people expect to take money out of the bank without having made any deposits. Walking to the bus, taking the stairs rather than the lift and doing some sort of weekly exercise is the minimum requirement for being fit – for the office.

To be fit for skiing and make the most of every precious moment spent in the mountains, we need to do a bit more to tune our vehicles. Apart from minimizing the risk of injury and spoiling our chances completely, fitness for skiing has some less obvious benefits. After all, it is not a bad idea to be really fit for life, is it? To learn how to relax and cope with stress, to become more aware of our bodies and to be able to focus our attention. Skiing offers the carrot that will help us to overcome the inertia so commonly experienced about taking exercise.

There is no way that anyone can make you participate in this chapter. However, if you are really committed to improving your skiing, having more fun and performing more consistently, then I recommend that you invest some time in preparing your body so that it can fully express its potential. If you decide not to participate, then please recognize that you have made that choice and realize that perhaps your inertia has got the better of you!

APPROPRIATE POSTURE

In chapter three we had a look at the ideal posture that we need to adopt for maintaining balance and creating or generating power in any athletic pursuit. Sadly we can only be as dynamic as our basic posture allows, bringing to skiing all the imbalances and structural weaknesses that have accrued over the years. Repetitive misuse of the body through slouching, the after-effect of injuries, when non-elastic scar tissue, stiffness, calcification or muscle spasms restrict movement, as well as the consequences of gravity as we age, all take their toll on our structural fitness.

When I was competing in freestyle skiing, my body had to develop a much greater range of movement, endurance, strength and power to be fit enough to withstand the hours of training that were necessary as well as the agility and versatility that the three events (ballet, moguls and aerials) demanded. Now, as I approach 40, I am no longer fit for ballet or aerials but continue to increase my range of movement and fitness for general skiing. It is possible as an adult to make considerable improvements, to let go of some of the 'history' that we tend to carry with us in our bodies and to minimize the inexorable pull downwards that gravity exerts on us, day after day, year in year out.

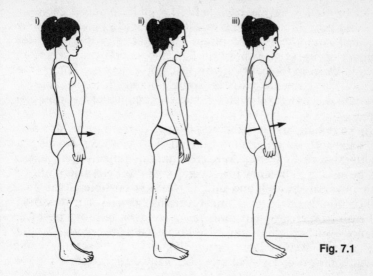

Fig. 7.1

Firstly, you need to familiarize yourself with the way you stand. Do you have a vertical alignment that maintains your body in the best position to function efficiently? Figure 7.1 shows the ideal and the two extremes: a hollow or overly flat back which may inhibit your skiing. You can stand against a wall and discover which is true for you.

To raise awareness of your posture and discover how it affects your dynamism, do the following exercise. Stand up with your ankles and knees flexed. If you have a mirror, stand sideways to it and watch the reflection. Let your pelvis tip backwards, creating a hollowed back – *voilà, la position toilette*! Now use your stomach and buttock muscles to tilt the pelvis to the other extreme, smoothing out the hollow. When you do this, don't clench the buttocks, instead let them spread sideways by extending the tailbone down and lifting the pelvis up by using the stomach muscles. Many women who frequently wear high heels find this particularly difficult. If you come into this category, then the stretching exercises will be particularly beneficial for you.

With the legs flexed, repeat these extremes and feel how soggy and powerless the legs feel when you have a hollow back and how much stronger they are when the pelvis is tipped upwards. It is as if all our power goes shooting out in the direction of an imaginary tail when the back is hollow and the power can only be effectively directed down our legs when the pelvis is tipped upwards slightly. Repeat these extremes and discover for yourself an in-between position that allows you to move more athletically from the balls of your feet. For effective skiing and to protect the vulnerable lower spine, we need to be able to maintain this pelvic tilt even when under emotional and physical stress.

By stretching and lengthening the spine, freeing the hips and the legs and strengthening the muscles, you can develop a posture that really works. Annie Sarson, a qualified yoga teacher, has been using stretches for several years to help skiers utilize their physical strength and mobility to best possible advantage. The section on 'stretching', incorporating her views, is designed to help you increase your range of movement, improve posture, balance your structure and raise kinaesthetic awareness. In the subsequent section, on 'strengthening', I describe some strengthening exercises that are specifically designed for skiing.

STRETCHING

Traditionally, training for various sports and athletic activities prepares the body for that specific activity. A footballer or tennis player will develop the parts of the body which are appropriate. Any sporting activity, whether for recreation or competition, is so much more effective when the whole body is involved. The asymmetrical development that can result from training to be fit for only one sport can damage your health and structural well-being in the longer term. However, skiing, like swimming and some track sports, involves the whole body, so total conditioning is required.

We need a sense of awareness of what each part of the body is doing, or about to do, from the toes up to the crown of the head, and to be able to let go of unnecessary tension. How tightly do you hold on to the car steering wheel when you are overtaking, or the telephone when making a difficult call? In how many situations do you find your teeth clenched or your shoulders hunched? It takes energy to do these things and perhaps this energy could be used more effectively elsewhere. Instead of sending messages to unnecessary muscles and burning up fuel, we can allow our energy to flow more freely through our bodies.

There is an alternative to the 'running upstairs ten times' and the 'sitting against the wall until your thighs burn' type of exercise. It is no short step from the kitchen sink or the office desk to effortless and graceful ski turns down your favourite mountain, so, if pumping iron and aerobic exercise are daunting, try the softer, alternative approach which you can practise at home. That's not to say that these stretching exercises are all easy, but if you put your mind and body to a daily or even three times weekly session you will feel stronger, more mobile and more relaxed as you approach the mountain – and the washing up! They can condition the whole body and at the same time raise awareness so that the body and mind are working in harmony, each enhancing the other.

Our bodies are much more adaptable than we think. After all, they have adapted to walking from home to car to office desk when once they used to hunt dinosaurs for supper. This adaptability can be put to advantage to loosen up tense and tired muscles and joints.

Wherever you are on the time scale, at the age of 20, 40, 60 or more, changes are possible and beneficial. Some teenagers are considerably less mobile than some of those who have achieved half a century. A mobile body gives a new freedom by allowing oxygen to circulate and energize parts of our bodies that we might not even have known we had.

As we mature, our bodies gradually fall out of alignment and develop postural imbalance as certain patterns of movement are favoured over others. Being right or left-handed means that we tend to move and use one half of the body more than the other. We also have habits like carrying a bag over one shoulder and activities such as tennis or golf which work one half of the body differently from the other. Skiing, unlike many sports, is a balanced activity. In other words the body needs to be able to move symmetrically, turning both to the left and to the right with equal facility. Skiing provides us with a unique opportunity to notice any lateral bias and balance it out. Most people find that they can turn one way better than the other, favouring one leg and always stopping and starting in the same direction. Stretching exercises will help you to strengthen the weaker side and even out any differences so you can become more balanced and versatile on the slopes.

The magic shoulder

To give you an experience of how easy and beneficial stretching can be, have a go at the following exercise.

1. Stand sideways to a wall, an arm's length away, stand straight and firm with your feet firmly placed hip width apart and toes pointing forward. Put the palm of your hand firmly to the wall with the fingers pointing upwards.
2. Imagine there is a layer of glue attaching your hand to the wall. Now you must put your imagination to use! The wall is very slowly falling away but your hand is still stuck to it and your feet are still firm on the floor, body upright. The shoulder joint opens and releases the arm. The game is not to push the wall but let it pull the arm. Let it happen while you count slowly to thirty.
4. Very gently unstick the glue from your hand and let the arm drop slowly down.
5. Lift both arms up in front of you – is one longer than the other? Now even them up by repeating on the other side.

The emphasis of the stretches is not on achievement. How long or how far you can go, doesn't matter. Its simply the effectiveness of doing them. It is important to let go of the feelings, 'I can't reach that far', 'My muscles aren't strong enough', 'I can never get my body into *that* shape' and the classic, 'I can't even touch my toes!' There are ways to touch your toes as you will find out! Before we begin with the stretches, a few words about feet, knees and breathing – all useful for living and essential for skiing.

FEET

These two things we pad about on and expect to last a lifetime are usually forgotten until they start objecting through lack of love and care. 'Out of sight, out of mind' is such a true saying. Poor old feet! Remember that wonderful feeling of release after the struggle to be free of the ski boot. Feet are hardworking yet they are perhaps the most abused part of the body. How about giving your feet the same attention as your hands? Treat them to an occasional massage and manicure. Keep your toenails short and when skiing always wear clean socks – the salt from sweat can cause discomfort.

Take your shoes and socks off now and feel the floor with the soles of your feet. How is it? Is it hard, soft, warm, cold, rough or smooth?

Stand up with the feet hip width apart and the toes facing forwards. Feel if your weight is evenly distributed between the left and right. No hurry, it takes a little while to bring your awareness to any specific area. Equalize the weight, if necessary, and notice what other adjustments the rest of the body has made to compensate.

Now make the *outsides* of the feet parallel (this is also the start of all the standing stretches we'll do later) and notice how the leg muscles activate and the back of the pelvis stretches to the sides. If the arch muscles of the feet are all active, there are three noticeable points of contact on the floor: under the big toe joint, the little toe joint and towards the back of the heel. See which of these three points has the firmest contact. Is there any difference between the left and right? What could you do to equalize the balance, not just left and right but all three contact points.

Have a look at the undersides of your shoes sometime. You will see the same areas of wear on all your shoes. This will give you direct feedback on how you use, or misuse your feet when you walk.

KNEES

The knee is the largest joint in the body, a simple hinged joint but with attachments that can cause problems. The front thigh muscle, the longest in the body, contracts easily and this can put strain on the ligaments and cause unnatural twisting. Contraction of the thigh muscle in skiing puts a heavy load on the knee and injuries are very common. In chapter eight Sarah explains a strengthening exercise specifically for women who, because of the inclined femur, need to balance the development of the thigh muscle. A thigh muscle which can stretch as well as contract will relieve the knee ligaments of overstrain as well as preventing stiffness.

'Swayback legs' is the dancer's term for a condition in which the knee joint is overextended. In some people, when standing, the shin bone slopes backwards, the calf muscles bulge out and the knee is overstretched at the back. To overcome this, the knee cap needs to be lifted up by the lower thigh muscle. A few people have the reverse of 'swayback legs', that is they find it impossible to straighten the leg completely. Here, the calf and the hamstring (back thigh muscle) need to soften and separate away from each other, allowing more space at the back of the knee.

BREATHING

From our first breath to our last, the body is programmed to ventilate automatically. We tend to interrupt this process by holding on to our breath and not letting it flow in and out, thus inhibiting the natural circulation and body rhythms. The breath not only carries oxygen to the muscles but also to the brain, which in turn sends messages to each part of the body. By increasing our intake of oxygen we clear the mind and speed up our metabolism and the rate at which energy is made available.

Generally when practising the stretches we need to breathe in smoothly, not forcefully, and then to extend into the movement on the exhalation (outward breath). Breathe evenly while making further adjustments and extensions and then inhale (breathe in) as you come out of the stretch. This is a natural breathing pattern that will automatically seem right. As you become more familiar with the poses, you can put more awareness into your breathing and let it do the stretching for you.

BEFORE YOU BEGIN

Where to practise
You will need enough space to stretch to the sides, front and back. It is better to practise these stretches with bare feet so that the soles of your feet are in contact with the floor, and a firm surface will assist in balancing better than a deep-pile carpet.

What you will need
You will need either a window sill or an upright chair at about hip height for support. For the sitting stretches you may need a large book - a telephone directory is ideal – or a folded blanket. A non-slip mat is very useful to anchor the feet.

How to practise

** Warm muscles stretch more easily than cold ones, so make sure that you are warmly and comfortably dressed.

** Wear loose clothing so you are not restricted.

** Practise the stretches in the order in which they are presented.

** Stretch both sides of the body evenly.

** Do not practise immediately after eating. Leave two hours after a heavy meal and one hour after a light meal.

** Look at the illustrations as well as the text for guidance.

** When you have finished stretching, lie down even if just for a couple of minutes so your body can assimilate its new alignment.

** Schedule regular short practices. Three twenty-minute sessions per week are more beneficial than one extra long session.

How to stretch

These stretching exercises may seem slow and meticulous, but the idea is to become more aware of your body, feeling movement in some detail and paying attention to the quality of your breathing. This will help you to focus the attention when it comes to skiing and maybe put you at the wheel of a finely tuned sports car instead of a rusty old banger.

How long should you hold each stretch?

This will vary from stretch to stretch. You will find some easier to hold than others. Never hold a stretch if you feel stuck in it. Always feel that you can adjust and lengthen.

Beware of bouncing

Many people think that in order to increase the range of movement it is necessary to bounce and jerk in a stretched position. This is extremely dangerous and can tear soft tissue. If a muscle is subjected to unusually rough treatment, it will contract rather than stretch, so bouncing actually defeats the purpose. Muscles are like elastic – they will give better service if they are gently stretched and released. So please be sensitive to what you can and cannot do. Feel the difference between a stretch and a strain. Do not use force. Trust your body to release, soften and lengthen through gradual, gentle stretches and the power of your awareness.

HEALTH WARNING! – **If you have any chronic structural problems, such as back trouble, please take medical advice before you start.**

STRETCHING EXERCISES

The ripe plum

1. Place your hands on the window sill or chair-back and step backwards about 1 m (3 ft), so that your legs are straight and you are bending forwards at the hips. Make sure that your feet are pointing forwards and are hip width apart.

2. Make a right angle with your body, keeping your back flat like a table top, your arms stretched out towards the back of the support and your legs firm (i).

3. Extend and open the backs of the knees, knee caps lifting, and pull up on the front of the thigh muscles. As you do that you can feel the hips extending back and away and the spine lengthening.

4. Allow the armpits to open downwards towards the floor, keeping the back flat and the legs firm. Don't let the front ribs sink down too much as this hollows the spine.

Fig. 7.2(i)

5. B R E A T H E   E V E N L Y. Gradually you will feel the spine stretch and lengthen and you may find it possible to move your feet further away from your support to give more space for the spine to stretch. Feel the feet firmly in touch with the floor and the legs strong. No bouncing; just let the muscles gradually stretch and extend.

6. Check that the right side and the left side of the body are stretching evenly.

7. Now walk your feet a step forward, allow the knees to bend a little, let go of the support and hang forward from the hips, allowing the upper body to come right down and the crown of the head to drop towards the floor, arms hanging loosely (ii).

8. Feel how the weight of the upper body allows the hamstrings (the back of the thighs) to stretch. Hang loose and breathe.

9. Now gradually straighten the knees so that the hamstrings stretch more. Let the upper body be still and heavy. Imagine your legs are tree trunks, firm and strong, and your upper body is a ripe fruit hanging off the tree (ii).

ii)

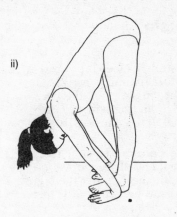

Fig. 7.2(ii)

10. B R E A T H E   E V E N L Y. Feel the stretch and let the outward breath release the muscles evenly on both sides.

11. To come up, breathe in, flex the knees slightly, place your hands on your hip bones and extend the crown of the head forward. Imagine a great hinge at the hip joint and raise the upper body, keeping the spine straight (iii).

Fig. 7.2(iii)

The mountain

1. Stand straight, feet hip width apart, toes pointing forwards with the outsides of the feet parallel. Standing with the feet like this allows the legs to be more active.

2. Feel the floor under your feet. Can you feel three points of contact, the heel, under the big toe joint and under the little toe joint?

3. Is your weight evenly distributed between the left and right foot?

4. Allow the backs of the knees to open, lifting the knee caps and the front thigh muscles.

Fig. 7.3

5. Let the lower spine stretch down, the tailbone moving down. Lift up out of the waist, left and right sides together, keeping the tops of the shoulders down.

6. BREATHE EVENLY.

7. Stretch the back of the neck, letting the crown of the head rise towards the ceiling. See how much space you can make between the shoulders and the ears.

8. Let your arms hang loosely. Feel your feet placed firmly on the floor and your energy lifted.

This exercise may help you to learn more about your body, and in time you will become more aware of shape and balance. It requires attention to detail, but you will soon remember the points to be aware of. This is a stretch that you can do at any time during the day and is particularly useful if you are having to stand for any length of time.

The dog pose

1. Kneel down on all fours, toes tucked under, feet and knees hip width apart.

2. Lift up the hips as high as you can; your heels will be off the floor. The palms of the hands are firmly in touch with the floor with the fingers pointing forwards.

3. Extend and open the backs of the legs and gradually let the heels come down towards the floor, but keep the hips high (i).

Fig. 7.4(i)

4. The spine stretches and the chest opens and moves towards the knees. Let your head hang freely from the neck and don't allow the shoulders to hunch up.

5. From this position, lift the head, lift the chest, bend the knees and bring them to the floor. Then lower the chest to the floor between the hands.

Fig. 7.4(ii)

6. Straighten the arms, lift the head and chest and bring the spine and legs off the floor. Check that the feet are still hip width apart and the hands are directly under the shoulders.

7. Allow the chest to travel forward through the arms (iii). Don't tighten the buttocks; let them spread sideways.

Fig. 7.4(iii)

8. Rest after this stretch by kneeling, relaxing forwards with your head on the floor.

The arrow

1. Place the feet about 90-120 cm (3-4 ft) apart. Start with the toes pointing forwards and the outsides of the feet parallel, remembering the three points of balance.
2. Take the arms out to the sides at shoulder height, palms facing down (i).

Fig. 7.5(i)

3. Turn the right foot out to the side and the left heel back at about 45 degrees (ii). This careful positioning of the feet makes a difference to the movement of the legs and upper body.

Fig. 7.5(ii)

4. Bend the right leg, lowering the right thigh to make a right angle with the lower leg (iii). You'll find that the left knee wants to bend too – see if you can keep it straight, which will stretch the hip joint.

Fig. 7.5(iii)

5. Place the right elbow on the right knee and let it rest there. Keep the left leg straight and firm.

6. Take the left arm straight up and over your left ear with the fingers pointing diagonally towards the ceiling. There is now a straight line from the outside of the left foot all the way up the left leg, left hip, left ribs and left arm to the fingertips (iv). You may notice that your right thigh has lifted; lower it back down to make a right angle with the lower leg.

Fig. 7.5(iv)

7. B R E A T H E   E V E N L Y. Let the upper body sit between the two legs, allowing the undercarriage to lower.

8. To come up, firm back on the left foot, straighten the right knee and bring the body back to a standing position, feet forwards, the arms hanging by your sides to rest.

9. Take a couple of breaths and repeat on the other side.

Alternative 'arrow' side bend

This side bend is easier when done against a wall. You don't actually stretch as far down, but the front body and hips really open up and get a good stretch.

1. Have your back to the wall, with your feet about 15 cm (6 in) away and 90 – 120 cm (3 – 4 ft) apart as before.

2. Do the stretches in exactly the same way but keep both hips, the shoulders, arms and back of the head in contact with the wall all the time. Can you feel how the chest opens?

Forward bend

1. Place your feet hip width apart with the toes pointing forward.

2. Lift up out of the pelvis but keep the shoulders soft.

3. Imagine there is a hinge through the hip joints and bend the upper body forwards from the hip joint with the spine straight.

4. Keep the chest lifted and let the crown of the head describe an arc as you come down. Let the arms hang loosely.

5. B R E A T H E   E V E N L Y. Relax the upper body, remember the image of the ripe fruit and refer to fig. (ii) on p.151. The legs can be a little bent or, if you want a more intense stretch, straighten them. If you feel

reasonably comfortable with straight legs, you'll find it easier to soften and relax the upper body, but go easy on the hamstrings if they are feeling tight. Don't push or strain. Let yourself hang loosely, allowing the body weight to lengthen the spine.

6. To come up, place your hands on the hip bones and lift the head and chest. Open the hinge at the hips, coming up with a flat back. (Refer to fig. (iii) on p.152).

The squatter

1. Place your feet about hip width apart, toes pointing forward.

2. Squat down so that your arms hang between your legs.

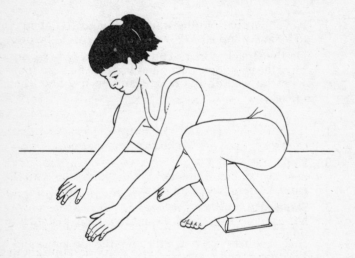

Fig. 7.6

3. Sit back so that your heels stretch down towards the floor, being careful not to fall over backwards. Some people can do this easily; if you can, bring your feet closer together to increase the stretch in the ankles and lower legs. If you find it difficult, place a book (telephone directory) under your heels and stretch down on to that.

The stork

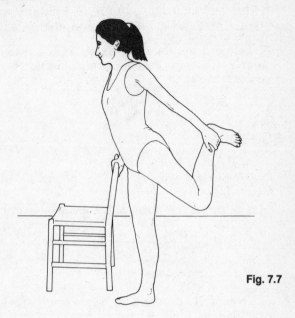

Fig. 7.7

1. Place a chair by your right side so that your right hand can rest on the back of the chair for support.

2. Stand on the right leg, bend the left knee and take the bent leg behind. Catch hold of the left ankle with the left hand, keeping the thigh vertical.

3. Stand firm on the right foot and leg and push away the left hand and the left foot until you feel a stretch in the thigh.

4. Keep the upper body facing forwards and upright to give you more of a stretch.

5. B R E A T H E   E V E N L Y, gradually letting the thigh stretch further.

6. Release the leg and bring the foot down to the floor.

7. Repeat on the other side.

8. B R E A T H E   E V E N L Y. Soften your focus for better balance.

Kneeling thigh stretch

WARNING! If your knees are painful, miss out this stretch and just practise the previous standing thigh stretch.

1. Kneel down on the floor. Sit on a book placed between your feet, keeping the back straight. Lift up from the base of the spine (i).

Fig. 7.8(i)

2. If you feel comfortable (i.e. your knees are not complaining and you would like to stretch the thighs more), remove the book and sit down on the floor. Lift up again from the base of the spine Fig. 7.8(ii)

Fig. 7.8(ii)

3. The third stage is to lower yourself backwards to rest down on your elbows. Your knees may lift up a little now, and the thighs will get a really good stretch if you gradually ease them down (iii).

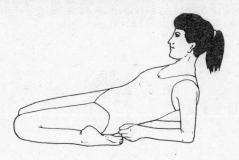

Fig. 7.8(iii)

4. A few people have naturally stretchy thighs and will be able to lie right down. Some firm support under the shoulders will help. B R E A T H E   E V E N L Y, softening the stomach muscles and letting gravity do the stretching for you (iv).

Fig. 7.8(iv)

5. However far you can stretch, stay in that position for as long as you feel comfortable, maybe two or three minutes.

6. To come up, reverse the sequence and then gently bend the back forwards from the kneeling position.

Sitting twist

1. Kneel on the floor and then move the left hip sideways on to the floor so that both legs are on the right, the knees are bent and the feet face the rear (i).

Fig. 7.9(i)

2. Sitting on the left hip, put the right hand on to the left knee and rest the fingertips of the left hand on the floor behind you to the left.

3. Still facing forwards, lift the upper body.

4. Keeping the left hip still, move the upper body and spine round to the left (fig 7.9(ii)). Imagine your spine is a corkscrew, lifting and turning from the very base of the spine right up to the crown of the head.

Fig. 7.9(ii)

5. BREATHE EVENLY. Keeping the back of the neck long, hold the twist for a moment and then lift and stretch a little more.

6. Turn to face forwards.

7. Repeat on the other side.

Hip Loosener

This stretch will help to loosen the hips. You may need to sit on a telephone directory to encourage the hip joints to start moving.

1. Sit cross-legged with the feet about 30 cm (1 ft) away from the hips and the soles of the feet facing the opposite sides of the room, each foot being under the opposite knee. The calves and the thighs form a triangle (i). Keep the feet away from the body; this stretch does not have the same effect if they are close in.

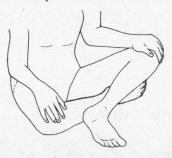

Fig. 7.10(i)

2. Lift up from the base of the spine, keeping the shoulders relaxed.

3. Lean forward, keeping the spine straight, and place the palms of the hands flat on the floor in front of the feet (ii).

Fig. 7.10(ii)

4. Relax the knees down. They will want to come up as you lean forward.

5. Keep lifting the spine from the base and walk your hands a little further forward. Again lift the spine.

6. B R E A T H E   E V E N L Y. Relax the knees down.

7. When you get to your maximum position forward, relax your head down and stay there for a few moments – you will feel a stretch deep in the hip joint. This can be quite a strong sensation as our normal hip movement is very restricted in daily activities.

8. Breathe into the hips, exhaling, softening and allowing them to move.

9. Come up and cross your legs the other way and repeat the movement. You will notice that one hip tends to respond more than the other. Just remember to relax the knees down and breathe.

Sitting forward stretch

1. Sitting on a book, stretch the legs out in front, with the toes pointing upward and the heels stretching away.

2. Lift up the spine, feeling it stretch upwards from the base to the crown of the head. Imagine a silver cord suspending you from the ceiling, lifting you upwards (i).

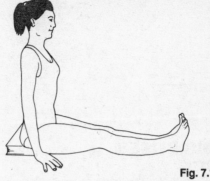

Fig. 7.11(i)

3. Let the knees bend a little. Reach forward with the hands, bending forward from the hips. Remember the image of the hinge running from the left hip to the right hip.

4. Place your hands on your shins, wherever comfortable. A little pull with the hands will help lift the spine. If it is uncomfortable to reach any further, put a firm belt round the soles of your feet and hold it in your hands as you lift up (ii).

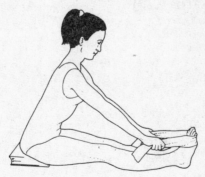

Fig. 7.11(ii)

5. Bend the elbows, still holding the belt if you are using one, and bring the upper body forward, letting the head

relax down (iii). B R E A T H E   E V E N L Y. If the hamstrings are tight, the knees can be bent a little.

Fig. 7.11(iii)

RESTING POSES

You may be pleased to know that rest and relaxation are an important part of stretching. If you have practised some or all of these stretches, you will probably be experiencing some unaccustomed sensations in your body. A few minutes of resting will help to assimilate the heightened awareness and let go of tension.

Legs up the wall

Fig. 7.12

This is a favourite among skiers. Lie on your back with your hips as close as possible to the wall. It is easier to get there from your side. Keep your legs straight with the heels extended and the soles of the feet facing the ceiling. Let your spine soften into the floor and breathe evenly, resting for five to ten minutes.

Deep relaxation

Fig. 7.13

1. Lie on your back on the floor on a blanket making sure you will be warm enough as the body temperature drops very quickly after activity. Start with your knees bent and feet on the floor, arms loose at your sides. Soften the back of the waist down and then extend the back of the neck, bringing the chin slightly down. Now gently straighten out one leg at a time without disturbing the upper body.

2. Do a body check starting at the feet and working upwards, letting each part soften and relax down in turn – feet, legs, hips, spine, arms and hands, shoulders, neck and head. Notice your body weight on the floor and breathe gently and evenly.

3. Your eyelids are softly closed and all the little muscles around the mouth and eyes and over the scalp are relaxed. Feel that the two sides of the body can slip further down and away to the left and the right.

4. Following your natural breathing pattern will help you to release the mind from its constant succession of thoughts and concerns. Be an observer, watching your breath. Allow it to breathe you; watch how and where the inward breath can fill the body. Follow it and then gently exhale and see how the outward breath can soften the joints and muscles. Your breathing is never forced but simply an extension of physical relaxation.

5. Always come out of relaxation slowly and gently and roll on to one side to come up. Five or ten minutes of this deep resting will refresh and energize the whole person,

mind and body. Sometimes it is hard to let go, but practising will make it easier.

STRENGTHENING

As Annie has explained, it is possible to strengthen your body without 'pumping iron'. I certainly agree that the stretching exercises she recommends do more than just increase mobility and improve posture. However, some people like to work at getting fit in a more traditional way so here is a series of strengthening exercises and suggestions for developing stamina, agility and power.

Strength is not just the ability to contract muscle tissue to control movement. Effective strength means having the ability to relax one group of muscles while tensing others. Strength must be balanced with relaxation. Strength without coordination is ineffective, because coordination means being able to move different parts of the body independently and with varying amounts of muscle contraction at will. Strength also requires reflexes which can start and stop movements in response to stimuli.

So, if you are one of those who eschew the stretching exercises because they seem too gentle, I would ask you to reconsider. The subtlety of the slow movements will help you to become more sensitive. Sensitivity enables you to learn faster as your body can feel awkwardness and inefficiency more quickly and can correct with greater accuracy and consistency.

Staying on top

I certainly recognize when I am off form and unfit for skiing. My perception of my ability to cope with demanding slopes and high speeds diminishes considerably. I literally don't 'have the stomach for it' or 'haven't got the guts'. My body's intelligence speaks through my emotions. When on top form and fit for skiing my confidence soars. So how about you? Have you got the stomach for it? There is no doubt that lack of fitness contributes to the majority of intermediate skiers' hiccups in learning and performance. Most people aren't fit for the office, let alone the demands of skiing all day in the mountains.

As we learn to slide and our skis accelerate, the body tends to get left behind. Adopting the anticipatory posture as described in chapter three will help us to balance and respond athletically. By strengthening the muscles in our abdomen, lower back and buttocks, this posture will be easier to maintain. Equally, as we become more proficient and ski faster over uneven terrain, we have to be able to create the greater forces that are necessary to resist the effects of higher speeds.

When skiing moguls, we need to flex and extend the legs to follow the contours of the terrain, thus keeping the feet on the ground and the upper body flowing smoothly. When absorbing a bump, we may get left behind in an ineffective compressed position. Were we to stay like this through the next hollow we would have no means of absorbing the next mogul, resulting in a rather uncomfortable ride. Know the feeling? Do you ever find that you get left in the back seat and your feet shoot out ahead of you? Similarly, in longer, faster turns some skiers 'open up' and become too tall between turns. Without sufficient strength in their mid-section they are unable to balance against the ski now under pressure. Both of these problems are largely caused by a body that is not sufficiently prepared for the demands being put upon it.

HOW TO TAILOR YOUR OWN FITNESS PROGRAMME

** It is a good idea to enrol a friend so that you can encourage each other and have some fun in the process.

** Bear in mind your age and current level of fitness.

** If you are very unfit and take no exercise, begin with improving your stamina by walking briskly, skipping, swimming or cycling. Be sensitive to your body: all you need achieve is mild breathlessness for about twenty minutes for the exercise to be effective. In this way you will improve the efficiency of your heart and lungs. If you overdo it, you will be less likely to want to continue.

** Success is a great motivator. So if, for example, you are able to walk a mile, swim two lengths or cycle three miles, time yourself, make a graph and plot your progress. Gradually increase the distance and speed as you feel able.

** Set yourself some realistic short-term and long-term targets.

** If you have no history of back ache or spinal problems, start doing the strengthening exercises three times a week, at least two months before you are going skiing.

** Remember that warming up provides your body and mind with a period of transition between inaction and action. By getting into the habit of warming up before becoming active you are more likely to be successful at whatever you attempt. Tuning in mentally means getting clear about what you want to achieve and preparing your mind for action.

STAMINA

Fatigue is the cause of many problems in skiing – injury, learning inappropriate patterns of movement and lack of enjoyment to name just three. You need endurance to be able to ski all day and take advantage of your time in the mountains, so time spent building stamina will not be wasted. 'Long', 'slow' and 'distance' are the key words to remember. Jogging, long brisk walks, swimming lengths and cycling during the summer months will build endurance. My favourite is riding a mountain bike around the Dorset hills. The downhill descent on this sort of bicycle requires similar visual and perceptual skills to skiing and some nerve!

AGILITY

It is essential to be able to move quickly in order to cope with fast changes of direction on steep slopes, narrow paths or in moguls. You can combine endurance with agility training in activities such as squash, dancing, football or badminton. I like to combine mobility with agility and play 'Hacky Sack', an American game of keeping a small beanbag off the ground for as long as possible. It takes a bit of practice to get the hang of the game but it is sociable, and the beanbag is small enough to carry around to play at any idle moment.

POWER

Power is the rate at which you can use muscular strength. To develop power it is necessary to work your muscles against a resistance and increase the speed of repetitions. If you want to develop greater power you should seek guidance from a qualified trainer at a gym where there are machines designed for specific muscle groups. Cycling up hills is a good alternative for developing powerful legs for skiing. Try a mountain bicycle – they are great fun.

STRENGTHENING EXERCISES

HEALTH WARNING! The lower spine stretches more easily than the middle of the back. Therefore it can easily be strained. It is important to do these exercises with this in mind and follow the instructions carefully. If you experience any strain, stop immediately.

** Before you start each exercise, read the explanation and study the illustrations.

** Warm up by skipping, dancing to some of your favourite music or running on the spot for a couple of minutes.

** Do the exercises in the order that they are presented.

** Don't rush the movements. Do them slowly and deliberately for maximum effect. It is not a race! Make the last repetition as good as the first.

** When you first do these exercises, make a note of how

many repetitions you were able to do without excessive strain.

** Gradually increase the number of repetitions.

** Warm down afterwards with some gentler exercise to clear the muscles of waste products.

Side leg lifts

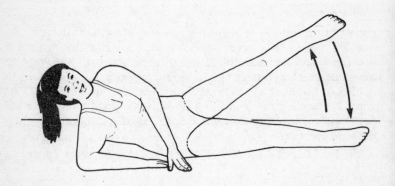

Fig. 7.14

1. Lie on your side with the lower arm supporting the upper body.
2. Flex the ankles so the toes are pointing towards the knees and the legs are firm and extending away.
3. Raise the upper leg towards the ceiling without rotating it. Keep the body firm, lowering the leg slowly. Maintain the tension in the leg and repeat.
4. Roll onto the other side and repeat with the other leg.

Sit-ups

1. Lie on your back with the knees bent and feet hooked under some heavy furniture or held by a partner.

2. With your hands behind your head, curl upwards with a rounded spine (i). **To protect the lower back, keep it on the floor for as long as possible.** Exhale as you come forwards.

Fig. 7.15(i)

3. Uncurl the spine, making contact with the floor with the lower spine first, rolling out until the shoulders meet the floor.

Fig. 7.15(ii)

4. Curl upwards as before, but this time bring your right elbow to your left knee (ii). Lower as before and repeat, bringing the left elbow to the right knee.

5. Repeat the sequence.

Back lifts

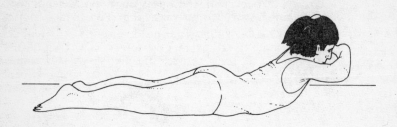

Fig. 7.16

1. Lie on your stomach and raise your arms to rest your wrists under your forehead with elbows bent.
2. Inhale as you raise your shoulders and arms, hold and exhale as you slowly lower them. Relax and repeat.

Leg lifts

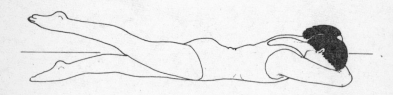

Fig. 7.17

1. Lie on your stomach, with the toes pointed. Extend the right leg away out of the hip joint, inhale as you raise the leg and hold for a few seconds. Lower slowly, exhaling and extending the leg as it comes down.

2. Extend the left leg, inhale as you raise and hold. Lower slowly, exhaling and extending the leg as it comes down.
3. Extend both legs, lift together, hold and lower while extending the legs. Repeat the sequence.

The curl

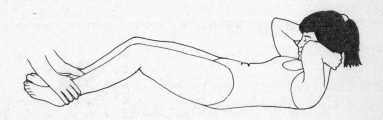

Fig. 7.18

1. Lie on your back with the knees slightly bent, hands behind the head.
2. Curl the shoulders forwards a little, keeping the lower back on the floor all the time.
3. Hold for a few seconds.
4. Relax and repeat.
5. To get up, first roll onto your side and then come up.

Mary Jo's buttock burn

Mary Jo Tiampo was World Mogul Champion in 1986. A diminutive Chinese American, she trained hard to build the strength to enable her to stay on the centre of her skis in the toughest terrain. Watching her train for this event was an eye opener. Here is the sequence of exercises she swears by to strengthen and tone the muscles that kept her on top.

In this exercise one leg works through all the movements before changing to the other. You will feel the supporting leg working hard as well. Start with six repetitions of each movement and, if you find that easy, increase the repetitions until you build up gradually to twenty. Doing the movements slowly and deliberately will have more effect than rushing them.

1.   The start position is on hands and knees (i).

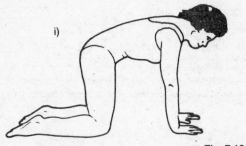

Fig. 7.19

2.   Bring the right leg up towards your chest (ii) and extend it backwards (iii) with the toe pointed. Repeat slowly for maximum effect.

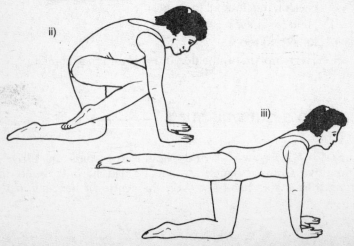

3. Return to start position. With the knee and ankle bent, lift the leg up to the side (iv), repeat slowly.

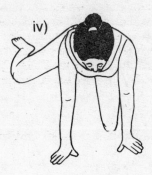

4. Return to start position. With the knee and ankle bent, lift the leg upwards (v and vi), lower slowly and repeat.

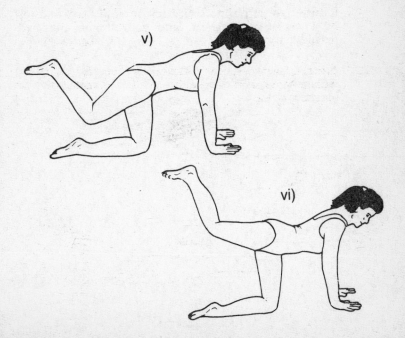

5. Return to start position. Bring the knee towards the opposite shoulder (vii) and then extend the leg diagonally (viii). Repeat slowly.

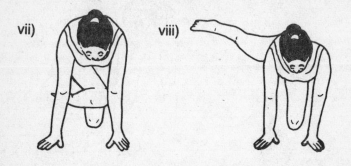

6. Return to start position. Change legs and repeat from the beginning.

7. Return to start position. Sit back on your heels and rest by lowering your chest onto your thighs, the arms extended forwards (ix).

The bridge

1. Lie on your back, with the hands placed flat on the floor by your sides. Bend the knees so that your feet are placed flat on the floor close to the hips (i).

Fig. 7.20(i)

2. Push into the floor with the hands and lift the hips as high as you can, leaving the shoulders and head on the floor (ii). Hold for a few moments. Rest and repeat.

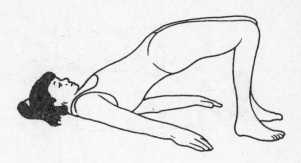

Fig. 7.20(ii)

3. Raise the hips as before and extend the right leg, keeping
    the right thigh next to the left thigh. Stretch the heel so
    that the toes are pulled back towards the body (iii).
    Breathe evenly, holding the leg up for as long as you can.
    Then lower the leg.

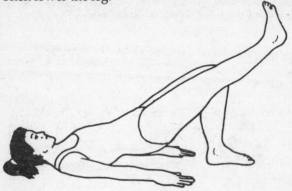

Fig. 7.20(iii)

4. Repeat with the left leg. You may want to lower the hips
    for a rest first.
5. Bring your knees up to your chest, holding onto your
    shins and let your spine relax onto the floor (iv).

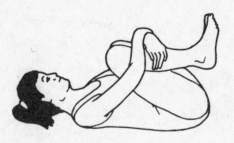

Fig. 7.20(iv)

6. To get up, first roll onto your side and then come up.

AVOIDING STIFFNESS

If you have not been taking much exercise and then embark on a fitness programme, you may experience stiffness in the muscles the following day. Likewise many skiers suffer from stiffness after skiing if unfit. The muscles in the legs tend to shorten as a result of repeated contractions and together with lactic acid, the waste product of expending energy, cause stiffness. The embarrassment of walking downstairs backwards to spare your aching thighs can be avoided.

** Make sure that you do not get overheated or chilled while skiing or exercising.

** Take the opportunity to have a walk afterwards.

** Loosen up with some stretches after a shower.

** The resting pose with the legs vertical, supported by a wall, (described in the Stretching exercise section) will also help to drain the lactic acid.

** Dancing in the disco is also good for loosening up the body, but beware of getting overheated and then chilled on the way home.

Stretching on the mountain

Many skiing injuries are the result of cold, tight muscles, tension and skiing without warming up. Both before the first run and during the day when you have been standing around, a gentle stretch will warm the body and put you in touch with the joints and muscles needed for effective skiing.

It always takes a little while to get both physically and mentally involved any activity. If I don't warm up before setting off down the slope, it takes me twice as long to feel tuned in. Warming up for a little while gives you a transition period when you can attune your body and your mind to the prospect of skiing. Please refer to chapter six for ways in which you can prepare mentally. Finding a level patch might seem obvious, but choose your spot carefully since even a slight gradient can cause problems while involved in a stretch.

WARNING: If you are a beginner, you may feel unsteady in exercises 6 and 7, so only do these once you have found your feet.

1. Lift the arms straight up, palms facing each other, fingertips to the sky. Standing firmly on the feet and legs, lift the upper body (i). Look up and say 'hello' to the sky, the clouds and the sun – whatever is up there.

2. Bring the arms to shoulder level, palms facing down and extend out to each side, allowing the shoulder joints to open. Extend the finger tips to the mountains (ii).

Fig 7.21

3. Keeping the arms extended, breathe in and on the outward breath rotate the body round to the right, keeping the feet still. Take a couple of breaths and notice the furthest point round that you can see. Breathe in and come back on the outward breath (iii). Repeat to the left and then lower the arms down. Repeat sequence three in both directions and notice if you can see further round this time.

4. To stretch the backs of the legs. Stand with the skis hip width apart, bend the knees and lean forward in front of the boots. Stretch the arms down towards the ski tips (iv). Place the hands down on the skis and relax the head down. Keep the hips high, the chest moving towards the knees, the hamstrings and calf muscles gently extending and the backs of the knees opening (v). For further stretch, bend the elbows and rest on your forearms, keeping the hips high (vi). Come back up with bent knees.

5. Leaning back in the boots, lower yourself as if into a sitting position and clasp the legs around the shins (vii). Drop the hips right down, still clasping the shins (viii). Lie right down on the snow – arms out to the sides, palms up. Let the mountain support the back and the head (ix). Take a few breaths of fresh air. To come up, reverse the process, moving the body weight forwards over the feet.

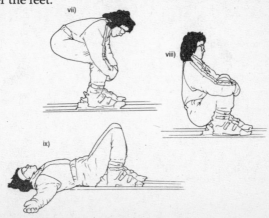

6. To stretch the legs and the hips. Using the poles for support, make a T shape with the skis, moving the left ski backwards to make the crossbar while keeping the back leg straight. (**WARNING: If the knee of the back leg feels *any* strain, do not continue with this exercise**.) Slide the right ski forward and allow the upper body to lower between the two legs (x). Let go of the tension in the right thigh so that the upper body can lower even further (xi). Keep the upper body as upright as possible. Repeat, using the right leg to form the crossbar.

7. To stretch the legs further. Stand on the left ski, poles forward for support, and lift the right ski, planting the tail in the snow (xii). Lift the upper body out of the pelvis and lean forward from the hip joint (xiii). Keep the head and shoulders soft. You may need to bend the knee of the lifted leg a little if the hamstring is tight. No straining or bouncing; just soften and breathe. Straighten up, bring the leg down and repeat on the other side.

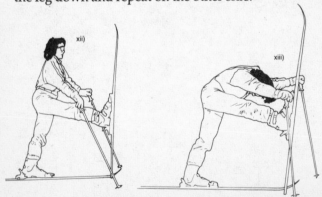

8. While the hips and the legs are easing themselves after the stretches, release the head, neck and shoulders by extending the back of the neck up and dropping the tops of the shoulders. Allow space between the ears and the shoulders. Then lower the chin on to the chest and gently rotate the head towards the right shoulder and then the left, keeping the chin down. Rotate forwards only, never backwards.

9. Finish with some hip rotations. With the feet slightly apart, make big circles with the hips, clockwise and anti-clockwise. Have the knees flexible but the upper body still from the waist upwards. Do it slowly and see if each circle can extend further than the last one.

10. Finally, do a body check to release any unnecessary tension that may remain. Legs, knees, hips, shoulders, arms, hands, neck, jaw and eyes. Breathe into the tight parts, let go of the tension and feel ready for skiing.

Chapter Eight

Vive la différence

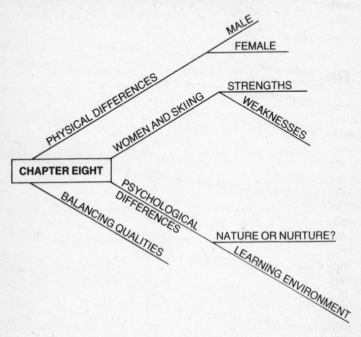

I have come across only two ski books written by women, amongst the dozens written by men. One of them, *The Centered Skier* by Denise McCluggage, spoke volumes to me. No other ski book, however interesting, ever had that effect. Perhaps it is because the book itself is balanced. Both male and female are taken into consideration without bias.

So it is with some hesitation that I begin this chapter. Although it is mostly about women, it will be of interest to both sexes. I am not a chauvinist. To me the healthy, balanced human being has access to characteristics of both sexes. The dearth of female viewpoint and values within the sport tempts me to open this can of worms; to say something about being a woman skier; to acknowledge and examine the female dilemma on the slopes; to point out the physical and psychological differences between the sexes; and to highlight the qualities that are available to both sexes.

As a professional female skier, celebrating my survival in an outdoor environment amongst a male majority, my minority voice will hopefully inspire other women to realize what is possible and encourage men to express more readily their feminine qualities.

ORIGINS

Skiing originated as a means of transport over snow-covered lands. The sport which evolved into today's downhill skiing has always seen more male participants and been largely dominated by men, although like riding and sailing it has always included women competitors. Indeed the last British World Champion was a woman, Evie Pinching, in the 1930's.

Unlike riding and sailing, where the horse and the boat diminish the sexual differences, in alpine racing separate women's events have emerged as a result of a woman's physiology. Men and women differ in several ways and a fair comparison is not possible when strength and power are the criteria.

If we look at the origins of ski instruction, it was clearly a man's game from the start, being first formalized in the armies of Europe. The infantry had to be mobile for winter warfare so they were simply lined up and instructed. In the cavalry, where 'cannon fodder' was also required at an alarming rate, the style of instruction was the same. Line up and do what I say. Discipline was more important than communication. The 'line them up and tell them who is boss' approach might be expedient for the instructor in the short term (as soldiers, short term might well have been all they got), but for the pupils it is not always the best method of transmitting information or the easiest to way to learn. Unfortunately, this style of 'teaching' still pervades many a ski-school class.

Women instructors were really only included in ski schools when recreational skiing brought an influx of small children into the resorts, and many must be congratulated for breaking out of the mould, introducing games and a caring, supportive environment for the very young in an atmosphere that was anything but. A small number of ex-racers were accepted as competent teachers for adults but still women remain in a minority. A ratio of 20 to 1 is not uncommon in some ski schools.

The comment 'you ski well for a girl' initially filled me with anger that it was not considered 'normal' to be a strong woman skier. I then realized that 'to ski like a woman' was actually a form of abuse in the ski world so I was actually being paid a compliment! In fact, it was comments like these that stirred me to look for answers to questions such as 'What *do* women ski like?' 'Why do so many drop out?' and 'How *could* women ski?'

PHYSICAL DIFFERENCES

For centuries muscular torsos and Rubenesque posteriors have captured the imagination of artists. These differences between male and female bodies are not just exaggerations or wild imaginings. They are determined by underlying differences of skeletal structure and weight distribution and have important implications in skiing.

There's no doubt that someone with a shorter stature, wider pelvis and lower weight-distribution will be more stable than a taller, narrower hipped, broad shouldered person with a heavier upper body.

Looking at the physical differences more closely, statistical averages are similar the world over with men turning out 7 per cent taller than women, the British woman being 1.62 m (5 ft 4 in) and the British man 1.83m (5 ft 9 in). Fully grown male dimensions are up to 10 per cent larger everywhere except the hips.

Women tend to carry about 14 per cent more fat than men and store it around the hips. Interestingly, the extra energy value is about 300,000 kJ, which approximately corresponds to the requirement for growing a full-term foetus. Evidently the survival of the species is more to blame for female curves than eating more or exercising less! If, like many, you fit the statistics but not your jeans, take heart, for you are more firmly planted on the planet and less likely to fall over. These differences in shape mean that women generally have a lower centre of mass and thus a better potential for balancing. The fact that in Olympic gymnastics only women compete on the balance beam illustrates this point.

So, in skiing women may have an initial advantage. However, men seem to make up for it with extra strength. They can often maintain an unstable posture for longer and then move their heavier upper bodies back over their feet to prevent a fall.

Whatever your shape, whether Eros or Aphrodite, it is possible to improve your ability to balance and to tip the odds on staying upright in your favour.

PHYSIOLOGICAL DIFFERENCES

The other physiological differences worth mentioning are:

** Men have a larger blood volume as well as a greater oxygen-carrying capacity within the blood itself. Although disadvantaged when exercising in the short term because of this, when longer-term endurance counts, women tend to utilize fat as fuel better and dehydrate less.

** Women are generally much more flexible than men, which allows for much easier movement and body flow while skiing. The female ligament structure is looser around the pelvis.

** Since women store at least 14 per cent more fat than men, they may be able to withstand the cold better. Now that ski clothing for women is more efficient and functional than it was a few years ago perhaps the myth that women feel the cold more than men can be put to rest.

** Because women have to produce more red blood cells on a regular basis each month, they seem to be able to acclimatize to altitude faster than men.

** There is evidence that women's muscles are less prone to damage.

A well-known exercise physiologist, Dr Craig Sharp, Director of the British Olympic Medical Centre, who has monitored the fitness parameters of various sportsmen and women, said, *'Women might outperform men only if the competition involved a cross-channel swim followed by a long run through deserts and mountains.'* In other words, women excel in endurance events and are more likely to survive situations of extreme deprivation. Hardly the way to describe a day's skiing but perhaps something to consider! The point here is not who is superior and who is inferior but what are our strengths and weaknesses and how do these affect our skiing?

Skiing, in essence, is the same for men and women. We are subjected to the same external physical laws of gravity and motion and use similar equipment. Having said that, and despite the fact that in my experience, when a couple take up skiing together, the wife usually makes more progress than the husband in the first few hours, the drop-out rate is much higher for female skiers than for male. Perhaps it is because nearly all ski teaching has been based on an analysis of the male physique and male psychology by men with men in mind.

WOMEN'S STRUCTURAL DISADVANTAGES

Although a wider pelvis and greater fat distribution in most women provide a lower centre of mass, they also create greater inertia in the limbs and lower trunk without the muscle to overcome it. Thus, once 'in the back seat' on a pair of skis, it is much harder for a woman to power herself out of trouble. A man, with his greater muscle strength and heavier upper body, can simply move his upper-body mass forward to regain equilibrium.

A greater hip width may result in an inherently more stable body shape but it also means that there is a greater incidence of knock knees among women. The child-bearing pelvis causes the thigh bones to angle inward towards the knees. Snowplough and stem shapes may initially come more easily for women than for men. That's all very well, you might say, but I want to ski parallel like all 'good' skiers. You may find that a little stem remains at the beginning of each turn or that the inner leg blocks effective edging and leg lean when skiing with the feet parallel. If you want to ski moguls and deep powder snow, a stem can get in the way of a quick pivot on a bump or cause problems in deep snow so versatility is ultimately the name of the game. Raising awareness of the inner leg and spending more time 'educating' the knee to turn uphill can ease this problem.

I had to spend hours practising the latter before taking my ski instructor's examinations. Any light showing between my lower legs would have surely failed me in compulsory demonstrations. I managed to eliminate the little stem 95 per cent of the time and wore baggy ski pants to minimize the effect of the remaining 5 per cent.

It is possible to ski parallel with your feet close together if you have this womanly trait of knock knees, but it does not provide a very stable base nor is it possible to change edges quickly. Watch the most efficient skiers in the world, the racers, and see if they keep their feet and legs jammed together while turning. I'm proud of my wider stance and my occasional stem on a steep slope as it aids stability, agility and, more important, it feels more natural for my body shape.

STRENGTHS AND WEAKNESSES

A woman's strongest muscles are in the thighs and as they develop through skiing a problem can arise in the knees. This is particularly important for active girls around puberty, who will find the bones changing shape and must adjust 'exercise' to cater for them. A woman's wider pelvis causes the femur (or thighbone) to incline inwards towards the knee. As a result of the inclined femur, the angle of the main quadricep (or thigh) muscle can pull the kneecap out of alignment and cause pain around the knee joint.

I have met women suffering from this condition who thought that their skiing days were numbered; they were delighted to find that some self-help could prevent early retirement. Given that any knee problem must first be examined by a doctor, if exercise is prescribed, the muscle towards the inner thigh, the *vastus medialis*, can be strengthened to balance the main quadricep development and stabilize the knee.

The following exercise (Fig. 8.1) is designed to do just that.

1. Sit on a table with the knees flexed. Exercise one leg at a time. Keeping the ankle flexed with the toes pointing up towards the knee, slowly raise the lower leg until it is *fully extended*, hold for five to ten seconds, lower and repeat. *The last 15 cm (6 in) of this extension are the most important.*

2.   You will be able to feel the *vastus medialis* contracting. When you find this easy hang a plastic bag containing a weight of 0.5 kg (1 lb) from the foot and hold for a longer period (ii). Increase the weight to 1 kg (2.2 lbs) and do half the number of repetitions when you find this easy.
     Change legs and repeat as above.

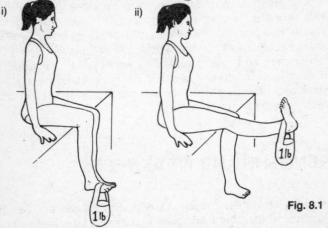

Fig. 8.1

If you have a weakness in the knee or have undergone knee surgery, consult your doctor and ask advice about a stabilized knee support. They are comfortable, keep the joint warm and give both physical and psychological support. There are several sorts available to suit the severity of the problem.

For both sexes, one of the major structural problems that can interfere with learning to ski is poor posture. The most common problem is a hollow or sway back, a pronounced curvature in the lumbo-sacral area when standing or lying on the floor. Women who habitually wear high-heeled shoes are particularly susceptible to this through a shortening of the muscles in the backs of the legs. In both sexes a hollow back is often exacerbated by weak stomach muscles which, in males, combined with a paunch, pulls the structure further out of vertical alignment.

Since the spine is at the centre of the body and the main support for the structure, any weakness will cause serious problems in skiing. Lower back pain is a very common complaint and its cause can often be attributed to continual and repetitive misuse of the body. The abuse does not always originate in the spine but in associated areas, such as in the legs, thighs, hips, stomach or shoulders, where stiffness or muscular imbalance can occur. Perhaps skis should carry a warning 'Skiing with a hollow back can seriously damage your health'. One can get away with participating in many sports with a hollow back but in skiing this curvature is vulnerable to all the shocks and compressive forces generated by a body in motion over irregular terrain.

The hollowness may only be a temporary reaction to stress as exhibited in *'la position toilette'*, where the pelvis tips downwards and the lower back stiffens, or it may be a more permanent curvature. When the pelvis tilts downwards, the legs are unable to function properly and the result is a loss of dynamism. A hollow back can be helped and sometimes completely corrected through stretching the hips and backs of the legs and strengthening the mid section of the body (stomach, buttocks and lower back).

Please refer to chapter seven for the stretching and strengthening exercises and chapter three for dynamic balancing.

PSYCHOLOGICAL DIFFERENCES – NATURE OR NURTURE?

Men are generally braver and more willing to take risks. As little boys they naturally seem to seek out the rough and tumble of life. Now whether this is as a result of social conditioning, being encouraged to test the limits of their physical ability, or of inherited traits is an argument that has yet to be resolved.

From my own experience as a woman it seems to be both. Women have a very different cultural heritage and we approach sport in a different way. We tend to be less competitive, more willing to admit fear and less confident in our athletic ability.

If the female body is clever enough to allow us 300,000 kJ of stored energy to grow a foetus, even if there is a shortage of food, perhaps it is also clever enough to protect the species for survival in other ways. Many women report that during and after ovulation and after childbirth they experience more anxiety and a consequent need for self-protection than at other times.

They describe feeling ultra-sensitive to all sorts of stimuli during and after ovulation. A heightened sense of smell, sound, vision and touch all contribute to a lowered threshold of stress tolerance. It seems we are in a receptive state in more than one way! Apparently women have a lower stress threshold at the best of times and exhibit more caution when confronted with risk, but when the body can or has conceived an awareness of the need for self-protection is more pronounced. I suspect that this is a biological fact and, when coupled with cultural conditioning, results in our traditional tendency to shy away from dangerous pursuits. On the other hand, the male, as the hunter, faced with all sorts of danger, had to evolve a psychology that would put the needs of the tribe even before his own life.

In many ways my upbringing did not encourage me to foster this feminine, instinct for self-preservation. Although the youngest, I assumed equality with my two brothers at an early age. Getting even was the name of the game and even though smaller and weaker, being included in their activities was important. Responding to their 'You can't play with us. You're just a girl' with 'I can and I'll show you I'm not just a girl' developed in me a determination to participate in the rough and tumble of life. Learning to ride a horse and competing against boys further supported my belief that I could perform on equal terms and even, on occasions, win. This belief was so unconscious that I would rarely doubt my equality or my ability to 'keep up with the boys'. Even as an adult I have automatically assumed equality in other activities, including skiing.

So is it possible for women to overcome moments of heightened perception of potential danger? I tend to treat myself with respect at those times and don't actively seek the extreme. When confronted with situations in which I feel ill at ease, a little self-reassurance usually calms me. After all my senses are working perfectly – too well in fact ! Having had conversations with several women who participate in high-risk sports, it seems we share the same approach, although this is by no means a conclusive answer to the question.

Obviously women aren't all the same. Personalities, bodies and past histories all vary considerably. However, certain tendencies do add up to a type or average which is worth having a look at.

** Little girls are encouraged to have an awareness of their bodies through early play and dance. Their sense of rhythm is usually highly developed and many have an awareness of sensuous movement from an early age.

** Many ski teachers report that women learn effective technique more quickly than men and attribute this to greater sensitivity, body awareness and rhythm.

** Women often tire more quickly when learning to ski. An American study concluded that this was because of excessive tension rather than weaker or less conditioned muscles.

If women can learn initial techniques so easily, why is it that they tend to get left behind on the gentler slopes as terminal intermediates while men forge ahead to advanced status?

One overriding factor seems to be that women expect less of themselves, often being referred to as 'under-achievers'. Elissa Slanger, author of *Ski Women's Way* believes that 'Because women approach skiing differently from men they bring different value systems to skiing.' For many women it is not the quantity but the quality that counts in skiing. The more quantitative values of speed and steepness just don't appeal as much as exhilaration, fun and sensuousness. It's the process rather than the result which counts.

Having successful experiences at the beginning will colour anybody's view of a sport but apparently boys are more likely to return to a task at which they previously failed. They ascribe their failures to 'bad luck', whereas women tend to ascribe failure to an accurate assessment of their current ability, allowing themselves to get discouraged. Once they fail, they are less likely to make further attempts.

This is where the style of teaching can make or break a woman skier. In many cases the need for a difference in attitude, a less competitive, more supportive learning atmosphere, goes unappreciated. Since women tend to relate to whole patterns of movement, rhythm and feeling, overly logical, analytical explanations may go over their heads and the use of certain words makes no sense.

Enter the square peg in the round hole syndrome. Take the example of the instructor who asks the female skier to be 'more aggressive'. It is an unfortunate word to choose as many women find the quality of aggression undesirable. They are at a loss when requested by an instructor to 'Attack the slope! Be more aggressive!' 'Do what?' she might ask, 'Do you mean beat the slope with my ski pole and growl?' Being unwilling or unable to generate this quality, she fails in both her own eyes and those of the instructor.

This gap in communication can be narrowed if we understand what is meant by 'being aggressive'. All it actually means is skiing with decisiveness, clarity and commitment. Paradoxically, that also means surrendering to the slope, flowing with gravity rather than avoiding it. When it is explained in this way, a woman can relate to the words and the slope and access the resources that she has readily available.

Women find it harder to take risks, to respond with action rather than inaction. We are often less decisive, less clear about planning a route and respond in a less determined manner to a challenge. By learning to make tactical decisions in route finding, to trust our bodies and technical ability, we can be encouraged to develop a more committed attitude. Commitment is a word that women can relate to.

It is not always necessary to use force to tackle a tricky slope. **Without the masculine muscular strength to power their way down, it is important that women spend time perfecting technique without stress, gaining real confidence on less difficult slopes, so that effective technique can be relied upon when on more demanding terrain.**

I know several women who cope in demanding conditions by using effective technique and sensitivity to make effortless turns, skiing softly and calmly, surrendering to the energy of the slope and using it to their advantage. In this way softness can overcome just as effectively as strength, if not more so in terms of energy expenditure. The saying *'maximum efficiency for least effort'* has always been my motto. This is truly a woman's way of skiing: no better or worse than a man's, just different.

EQUIPMENT FOR WOMEN

It is said that a poor workman always blames his tools. Many women would make a quantum leap in their skiing if only they did just that. Men tend to be more aware that good equipment will assist their progress and women often settle for less. When describing their ability, women are more likely to underestimate their level of skill whereas men are prone to exaggerate their prowess. But the ski shop personnel will fit equipment to the perceived level of competence. This poses no problem for the man, who can play a jig on his Stradivarius. For the woman, however, lower-level equipment will limit her ability to play beautiful music and discover her potential.

Fortunately, the ski industry has recently woken up to the fact that more than 40 per cent of skiers are women and are busy creating equipment to suit their taste and needs. Previously, many expert women skiers found it impossible to get a performance boot that would allow room for the lower calf muscle of the female leg, while providing adequate lateral support with a soft enough forward flex. Similarly, many lighter women skiers had to buy junior racing skis to match their high-performance characteristics and softer flex pattern.

Much of the equipment designed for women is sadly just a cosmetic job to appeal to the more fashion conscious. However, there are some ski and boot manufacturers who have taken the needs of women more seriously. A wide range of boots to suit the female foot at all levels of expertise means that comfort, fit and function are now available.

Becoming familiar with your own skis and avoiding the aggravation of sore feet from badly fitting rental boots makes it worth investing in equipment if you really want to make progress. Don't rush a purchase, particularly when buying boots. Take time to research what is available and don't be too modest about your aspirations and ability. Making an investment in skiing equipment is actually an acknowledgement and commitment not only to skiing but to one's self.

HOW TO STAY AHEAD

Although the physical strength differential has created segregated events in skiing competitions, I have found few occasions in my skiing career when I felt unable to ski alongside men. Even now, as I approach 40, I am still able to ski with experts of half my age. When you are flowing with gravity, you are playing with the same forces, and any strength differences can be evened out.

Relying on effective technique rather than muscle certainly helps. However, over the years I have also developed certain tactics that will help anyone who is afraid of being left behind – male or female! It is amazing how many people exacerbate the problem by putting themselves at the back of the group because they feel the slowest. Thinking that you can't keep up creates the feeling of being rushed and produces unnecessary tension thus wasting important energy resources. Perhaps the group *is* too fast for you, but before you give up use some of the following tactics:

** Always stay in the front of the group, either setting the pace or following the leader. This means that you have time to have a breather. There is nothing worse than arriving puffed only to see the group set off immediately.

** Clear the air by expressing your worry about holding the group up. Very often people are delighted to be able to enjoy the view while they wait for you to have a breather.

** Take special care to select your route. There are always more economical ways in terms of energy expenditure. This could mean taking a more direct route or making longer faster turns in more mellow terrain. So be clear about where you are going. Don't just follow blindly.

** Use the terrain to your advantage, choosing bumps and convex shapes to deflect off.

** Do not trade a well-balanced posture at a slightly slower speed for a speed that feels uncomfortable and that causes imbalance from holding back. Your legs will tire in no time. Stay at a speed at which you feel moderately comfortable and at which you can flow.

** When in moguls, choose a less intense line. Even ski the side of the run where there are fewer bumps. The saying 'Old freestylers never die. They just learn to ski the sides' is true in my case.

** Monitor your energy expenditure. Ask yourself the question, 'Am I wasting energy anywhere?' Do a body scan and let go of muscles that don't need to be tensed.

** Check your breathing. Is the effort of 'trying to keep up' causing you to restrict your breathing pattern?

If, after doing the above, you are still stressed and rushed, perhaps the reality is that you are not skiing fast enough to keep up with your friends and you would be more relaxed with people who ski at your pace. *View this as a temporary measure and not a final statement about your ability.* All you have to do is to improve your technique and ability to cope with speed and steepness and you will be able to join your friends again. But be clear that this is what you really want and that it is realistic. Perhaps all you want from skiing is to cruise around on mellow slopes and enjoy being in the mountains. *More and more women are discovering that skiing can be fun and satisfying at every level of expertise.* Instead of doing it because their partners do it, they are finding their own unique form of expression within the sport. By recognizing strengths and weaknesses, valuing our unique body shape, we can add some special qualities to the slopes.

Indeed, by recognizing the differences between men and women and respecting that we are neither all male nor all female but share many of each other's characteristics, both sexes can improve their skiing. In balancing strength with sensitivity and sensitivity with strength we can express more of our potential, more of our whole being. Generally women need to learn to take more risks and develop a more decisive attitude whereas men could benefit enormously from developing their more feminine qualities of sensitivity and grace.

Chapter Nine

The art of skiing

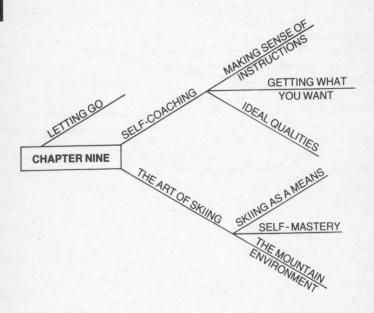

LETTING GO

The mind does not like letting go. After all, it believes that it is the boss and takes credit for everything. So who is going to run the show if it loses control? This sense of insecurity and separateness from the rest of the body is the way that the ego exerts its hold on us.

The most common symptom seems to be overattachment to results. It is a paradox that never ceases to amaze me. The moment you give up trying is the moment you get what you were wanting. Even in writing this book, letting go of my concern over finishing it, allows it to emerge from wherever it is coming from. My intention is to finish it; of that there is no doubt – particularly with a publisher breathing down my neck and a signed contract on his desk. My degree of commitment is high and with 60,000 words completed I have developed some trust in my ability to write. So there is a choice – to finish it or not to finish it. To go for it 100 per cent or doodle, procrastinate, make excuses, get sick and manipulate the fine print of the contract. Skiing is a bit like this. We can go for it 100 per cent or we can dither, hesitate and allow the mind to rule us.

So, having decided to go for the goal of completing this book, I am faced with all the concerns about how it will be received. Will it help skiers to get more out of their skiing, the mountains and themselves? If, because of these concerns, my attention was continually focused on whether I was achieving the desired result or not, I would never get a word on the page. Every word would have to be perfect as it was written, since it would have to live up to the demands of the final product. In constantly looking for a result I would lose touch with the source of inspiration, the self in the present.

Intention is the basic aim or purpose that moves us towards the goal. *It is essential to have intention and to have a goal but it has to be OK not to succeed. Being tolerant of failure does not necessarily invite failure. More often it creates space for success.* If we are afraid of failing, we seem to attract it like a magnet. We can foresee the direction of our progress but not its pace. If our awareness is tied up with concerns about reaching the goal, then the pure involvement in the activity is dissipated. By giving yourself permission to fail or by pretending in a race that this is just a practice run, you can detach yourself from being overconcerned about the result.

Someone once said that as long as you look after the nuts and bolts creativity will take care of itself. So I sit down with a short-term plan that will bring me closer to the final goal and start writing. It's the same in skiing. Once it is clear what you want to learn – go skiing!

If you have been participating in all the exercises as you read this book, you have probably made umpteen discoveries about your mind and body. The style of coaching has been to ask you questions and direct your attention rather than direct your actions. It is worth noting that the root of the word 'educate' came from the Latin *educare* = to lead forth. In 1603 its meaning was defined as 'to bring out, elicit, develop' and in 1979 it was defined as 'to train the mind and abilities of, to provide education for'. An interesting deviation in interpretation. You have probably realized that coaching is all about 'bringing out from within' rather than 'stuffing in from without'. This chapter helps you to consolidate what you have learned so far and suggests guidelines for the future.

HOW TO TURN INSTRUCTIONS INTO EXPERIENCES

When you go skiing, particularly if you are a beginner, you may want to go to ski school. After reading this book and starting to coach yourself you may find the style of communication rather different. When you are given an instruction to do something, the classic being 'Bend your knees', you have several choices about how to help your body to do that. If bending the knees was easy to do by simply giving an instruction, then everyone who heard the instruction once would be bending their knees. This does not seem to be the case. It is like the instruction in tennis 'Watch the ball'. How many times do you have to be told? Only when the ball becomes interesting – by asking questions about whether the ball is spinning and what you can see on it (writing, shadows, etc) – does the attention rivet itself on the ball. The watching becomes effortless and guess what? The body has both the feedback it needs to hit the ball and, with the mental chatter reduced, the freedom to coordinate fluidly.

If you have been doing the skiing awareness exercises, you may have already discovered that you favour a particular style of game. Personally, I prefer the imagery games but everyone is different and what words one day might not the next – particularly if you expect it to! Whatever you choose, stick with it for a while. Don't switch games too often. So, to recap: here are some different approaches that you could use to deal with 'Bend your knees':

   **   Ask yourself, 'What is he really after? How does this fit into active and dynamic balancing? Oh! He wants me to lower my mass. Now I understand.'

** Turn the instruction into a question. 'How much are my knees bending?' Follow the questioning process described in chapter five. 'When, where, how much?' Rate the degree of flex on the scale of 1 to 10.

** Watch the instructor's demonstration. Don't just watch his knees: watch the whole image – feet, ankles, hips and upper body – so you can put the knees into context with his whole shape. Use soft focus to do this. Other parts of his body may be bending too. Internalize what you see and visualise yourself doing it.

** Imagine something that elicits that movement, such as shock absorbers, rubber legs. Act out your image.

In this way you will be able to access your experience and feeling rather than getting hung up on the words, wondering how to interpret them into physical action.

GETTING WHAT YOU WANT

You might think that we have already covered this subject in chapter two but you may find it useful to refocus on what you wanted to achieve, check that it is realistic and notice if you have moved the goal posts. Very often when we raise awareness we find out that we actually want something different. That's fine; just notice that change and decide what you are aiming for now.

One of my clients, who was initially unwilling to get involved in some of the games, eventually told me she realized she had missed out earlier on in the week by only being 'half there'. 'By letting go and getting into my experience I discovered such joy in being committed, for once the result was irrelevant. Guess what? The result was there all the time. What I was really after was the joy but I thought the joy would come from the result, from skiing a certain way.'

I laughed and remembered a similar experience. When I became freestyle champion I expected to feel 'complete and satisfied'. I had been working hard for it but once it happened, nothing changed. What a lesson that was, and it took a while to learn it – that completeness or satisfaction originate here and now, not out there in a result. When we realize this, we can go for all sorts of goals with the detachment that comes from knowing that our sense of self is not dependent upon them.

DEVELOPING A SUPPORT SYSTEM

Share your self-coaching with a partner even if he or she is not actively involved. By expressing your discoveries you will make them part of you. You will probably ski with different people and notice their individual brands of self-interference. This can be distracting at times but avoid browbeating them with what you think they *should* be doing. Wait for the opportunity to arise, as it surely will, when you can share *your experience*. By that I mean what is actually happening in your learning. Communicate from your heart rather than your head. Once you begin to self-coach, you will be able to nourish other people and contribute to their growth in the same sensitive way that you do to your own, by asking questions, raising awareness and letting go of judgements.

You may have realized that the process of learning will carry on after you have finished this book, especially if you have adopted some of the suggestions and a style of self-coaching that suits you. Hopefully, you will continue to use the book as a resource. If you refer back to it and repeat the exercises, you will discover something new each time you do. That is the beauty of awareness. The game is always changing, always offering us something fresh and interesting to observe.

It is twelve years since I first became aware of the inner game and my excitement about expressing my potential never diminishes. There is always something to uncover, some resistance to overcome, a different quality to explore. We all contain seeds of every imaginable quality that will only sprout and develop if warmed and watered. Perhaps you can identify some inner quality in yourself that could be encouraged to emerge, given the right nourishment. The nourishment is of course awareness, trust and commitment.

The following exercise will help you to clarify the sort of qualities that you might want to express as a skier.

Your ideal

Write down five inner qualities that your ideal skier might exemplify:

....

....

....

....

....

Here is a list of the qualities that my ideal expresses; it may help you:

Awareness

Concentration

Relaxation

Detachment

Calm

Trust

Commitment

Responsibility

Confidence

Happiness/contentment

How much on average of each of your chosen qualities are you expressing in your skiing or in your life at the moment? To find out, rate them on a scale of 1 to 10 (1 = not at all, 10 = a lot). This simple exercise has clarified your ideal and raised your awareness of where you are now. The process of moving towards your ideal is already underway. Trust that your awareness will produce change. You don't have to try hard to achieve results.

It is helpful to make a graph for each of these five qualities so you can focus on them regularly and acknowledge your progress. Mark 1 to 10 up the side of the graph and your daily or weekly checkpoints along the bottom. When your 1 becomes a 10, acknowledge that you have reached your goal and set yourself another one. If you get stuck on, say, 8, ask yourself what you might have to let go of or do to make the 8 a 10. Be specific. How are you keeping yourself stuck? Another way of moving on is to make the 8 a 1 and let yourself envisage a new scale. You can do this simple awareness exercise at any time.

PARTICIPATION

At the beginning of the book I encouraged you to participate in the exercises and games. You might like to find out how much you have allowed yourself to get involved in the process. Obviously if you have not had a chance to do the skiing exercises you will not be able to rate them yet. The game here is to rate the exercises that you *have* or *could have* done. It is fine with me if you have not done any of the exercises; I don't mind at all. However, if you started out intending to achieve results and have not been willing to commit yourself, then you know who is responsible! All that is intended, once again, is to raise your awareness of your approach to learning. There are no right and wrong numbers, no good and bad scores. There is just what is.

1. Agony/ecstasy exercise (chapter 2)....................................
2. Personal profile questionnaire (chapter 2)...........................
3. Goal-setting questionnaire (chapter 2) ....
4. Foot awareness exercises (chapter 3) ....
5. Balancing exercises (chapter 3) ....
6. Balancing exercises (on skis, chapter 3)..............................
7. Centring exercises (chapter 3) ....
8. Centring exercises (on skis, chapter 3) ....
9. Relaxation exercise (chapter 4) ....
10. Tension-release exercise (chapter 4)...................................
11. 39 steps exercise (chapter 4) ....
12. Sensory exercises (chapter 5) ....
13. Sensory exercises (on skis, chapter 5)................................
14. Questioning process (on skis, chapter 5).............................
15. Magical Mystery Tour (on skis, chapter 5) ....
16. Now! (on skis, chapter 5)...

Work out an average of the exercises scored so far . . .

SELF-ACKNOWLEDGEMENT

You have to take responsibility for whatever you have achieved. It is amazing how hard this can be sometimes. Our ego either likes to take credit when no credit is due, thinking that it has 'done it all' or it denies success by saying things like, 'Well it was easy wasn't it?' or 'That was pure luck'.

So, if you have begun to improve your fitness and raise awareness, please acknowledge that *you* have. Perhaps you got in touch with some unwanted tension or anxiety and worked your way through it and gave yourself something more useful to focus on. Or perhaps you have begun to visualise. Please take responsibility for doing this. You may attempt to avoid responsibility by saying something like, 'Well, it was reading the book that did it', or 'The conditions were perfect. It wasn't really that hard'. If something is to become part of you, you have to own it. This is all part of believing in yourself and developing confidence.

Acknowledge that you have been willing to read the book this far and that you have participated . . . on average (refer to the above exercise). It is likely that this figure will correspond to the degree to which you have achieved what you wanted.

If you regularly acknowledge what you discover, it will help you to keep the momentum going. We all need encouragement but sometimes it is not available externally so it is wise not always to look outside yourself for support. The inner coach can recognize your efforts and give you an internal pat on the back.

You may think that visible external results are the only things worth acknowledging. As you get involved in the games and your awareness deepens, you will realize that in the internal game there is a multitude of victories worthy of note. This adds a richness to every experience and the opportunity to view the process as more interesting than the actual result.

BALANCING QUANTITY AND QUALITY

When I was a freestyle competitor, the pressure to learn new manoeuvres was intense. At every competition there would be new developments, and judges were always impressed by an original move. So between competitions I would learn more and more new tricks, paying little attention to practising what I already knew or simply enjoying what I could do.

Eventually I came up against a brick wall and nothing would go right – not even the old favourites. I was out of balance, unhappy and generally uninspired. This is an extreme example of what happens when we ignore the quality of what we are doing, the need to play and practise without 'going anywhere', and it is something worth bearing in mind if you ever feel stuck on a plateau.

At the other end of the spectrum some skiers might spend all their time on an easy slope, practising what they know until they have grooved a deep, comfortable rut. In any human activity the elements of learning and practice need to be kept in some sort of balance. When they get out of balance, eventually we lose our ability too learn new things and perform what we know with any consistency. To coach yourself effectively you will need to keep an eye on this. Are you primarily a learner or a performer? If the balance has tipped too far one way, your progress and enjoyment may be in danger so take action. You may find that you naturally flow in and out of these two modes and that there are periods of learning followed by periods of performance practice. Don't get discouraged. Sometimes these are natural plateaux. See them for what they are, part of the cycle of change.

ALTERNATIVES

One way to blow the cobwebs away and broaden your horizons is to bring some variety into your experience in the mountains. Downhill skiing is not the only way to enjoy flowing with gravity in the mountains. In the last couple of years mono skiing, snow boarding and telemark skiing have caught the imagination of the recreational skier and are becoming very popular. Mono skiing, with the feet placed side by side on a single wide ski, is easy to learn and although you may wish you had two skis when negotiating flat terrain, many resorts are ideally suited for this new form of skiing.

Snow boarding is more related to surfing and skateboarding than to skiing and although more difficult to learn in the initial stages than mono skiing, it provides an exciting alternative.

The Telemark, invented in the 1860s by Sondre Norheim, a Norwegian ski jumper, was the original ski turn. Performed with free heel bindings on narrow alpine skis this classic form of skiing is being revived worldwide. The leather boots are light and fix into a simple toe piece so that the heel can lift for walking uphill. The downhill turning position involves an elegant lowering of the inside knee to stabilize the body and prevent the skier from falling forwards. Telemark skiing requires sensitivity and a refined sense of balance and is perhaps the most difficult but rewarding of the alternatives.

Three years ago I began telemark skiing to provide myself with a new challenge. It was wonderful to be a beginner again, to fall frequently and to feel the joy of making progress. Now I use telemark skis to go touring far from the madding crowd and to explore balance in a different way.

Nordic or cross-country skiing is a different sort of alternative and one that I would recommend for a beginner. My niece and nephew spent their first morning on skis sliding around a cross country track, finding their balance and learning to be athletic in their movements. The environment is less daunting. The equipment is light, and the sensations of sliding forwards and being on top of the ski are easy to experience on flat terrain without the prospect of sliding too fast. Cross-country skiing is a perfect alternative when storms cause lift closures or bad weather makes skiing more like a survival test.

Take advantage of these alternatives and learn to balance on different equipment, adding variety and versatility to your repertoire.

REFLECTION

After a day's skiing it is worth reflecting on what happened and asking yourself two questions:

WHAT WORKED?

WHAT GOT IN THE WAY?

One of my clients, who shall remain nameless, kindly lent me her notebook as a resource for this exercise. Here are the things that she listed:

WHAT WORKED	WHAT GOT IN THE WAY
Feeling my feet	Self-criticism
Looking ahead	Tight pants
Floppy dolls	Thinking about lunch when not hungry
Trusting my skis	Thinking too much generally
Being a bird	Trying too hard
Singing	

On my ski course I encourage people to note down every evening what they discover during the day under those two headings. Many things we observe tend to get forgotten between skiing holidays, so this can help you maintain awareness and reinforce your learning. By rereading the notes before you go skiing again, you will recall all sorts of little details. For instance, the anonymous client above will remember that tight pants spoiled her enjoyment one day! Not a lot you can do about that once you are out on the slopes.

WHEN IN DOUBT - RAISE AWARENESS

So you are stuck. not clear what to do now, where to go, what to focus on and how to coach yourself. Whenever this happens, there are two simple questions to ask yourself which will bring you back in touch with yourself:

> WHAT DO I WANT RIGHT NOW?
> WHAT IS HAPPENING?

These two questions are your passport to progress.

THE ART OF SKIING

As a teacher, I feel I have a responsibility to point out to the uninitiated and inexperienced what lies beyond the nursery slope, to explain the art of skiing. There are no visible boundaries to this game. There is no obvious baseline or net cord. There is no time or place that you can say, 'I have scored or won the match' since *skiing is a means, not an end*.

It is an individual activity, and it begins within, with your body shape and type, your particular inherited characteristics and your unique personality. Whatever we bring to the mountains – whether one-legged and one-eyed, full-bodied youth or veteran status – skiing is a unique personal challenge. Nobody learns it for you, nobody can confront your fear for you and, nobody can take away your satisfaction and exhilaration at the end of the day.

This is not intended to put you off, rather to put you into the larger context of the art of skiing. Georges Joubert in his book

Skiing, An Art . . . A Technique states that 'skiing is more an art than a technique' and that skiing is 'the means to express the joy, harmony and communion with nature which you feel on the snow just as does the bird in the air'.

SELF-MASTERY

The way to master the art of skiing and harmonize with this adventure is through self-mastery. As a beginner sliding down a nursery slope the perceived level of risk is high. As a skier becomes more skilful, this feeling diminishes and his or her horizons broaden to tackle a blue run, then a red, then a red without falling, then a faster red, then an occasional black. In the process of becoming a complete skier he or she will seek out all conditions, steeper slopes or the most direct line, eventually venturing off into the real wilderness and facing the dance partner head on. Whatever your current level and whatever your aspirations, that is the possible ladder of progress. With modern equipment, teaching methods and the mileage that fast lifts provide this may take only a few weeks.

The mountain has its own rules. The lowlander's age-old romance with the single snowflake in its diversity and beauty paints for us an unrealistic picture of the nature of snow. The snowflake that falls out of the sky and enchants us as an independent free droplet of frozen water gains a mighty power once spread in deep layers over 3,000 vertical metres (9250 ft) of rock.

The pristine alpine world is both powerful and delicate. As outsiders, being in an environment so diametrically different from our own, we must recognize our responsibilities. Young trees, the forest of the future, are slashed by skis, mountain fauna run for their lives and local inhabitants risk themselves saving the tourist who, in his ignorance, has come face to face with the harsh reality of the mountain.

As a lowlander, cushioned by central heating, four-wheel drive, mountain restaurants, marked pistes and safety patrols, it is easy to be lulled into a state of unconsciousness. Any awareness and respect for this rugged but delicate environment is virtually lost. The danger is masked, veiled by the comforts of modern technology.

You may have learned a set of movement patterns called skiing that can get you around on a snow-covered mountain and read a book or two about avalanches and mountain craft. You may feel at one with the mountain from a deck chair in the valley, while admiring its majestic contours. Remaining at one as you mount its flanks and explore its secrets is a game that can cost your or someone else's life unless you learn to respect and understand it.

The element of risk in the sport of skiing is an issue between each person and the mountain. Without some risk, skiing would lose its appeal for the majority of skiers. In the words of Jean Marc Boivin, who thrives on extreme risk, having skied many steep slopes, including Les Drus (65 degrees) and the East Face of the Matterhorn (60 degrees):

> *He who takes no risk does not appreciate the true value of life – that is a completely banal path. All Alpinists, all skiers take pleasure in going beyond their own limits. Each one does so at their own level.*

> Powder Magazine (1989)

Getting to know your 'own level', taking complete responsibility for your actions and being able to express yourself within these parameters is true self-mastery. This is when you begin to glimpse the art of skiing. An awareness that is not dependent on technique and is just as available to the beginner as the expert.

THE POWER OF THE SNOWFLAKE

The power inherent in the mountains is perhaps not always appreciated. Just as on a liner in mid ocean we do not fully realize the power of the water and the waves so in a 'protected' ski resort we do not recognize the potency behind the snow, the wind and the combination of the elements at high altitude.

As you expand your awareness of the mountain environment, snow will begin to take on many different forms. The Eskimos have over a hundred different words for snow. There cannot be much else to discuss in the frozen wastes. As you learn to ski, you will begin to recognize a variety of textures underfoot that will affect your speed and balance. The snow will begin to take on a personality with swings of mood – light, heavy, dead and alive.

The type of snow that falls out of the sky depends on three things – temperature, humidity and wind. Once a snowflake settles, it begins a process that does not end until it is finally transformed into spring melt water. It may seem inanimate upon the ground but it is constantly undergoing changes as a result of the slope aspect in relation to sun, wind and pressure – the pressure of the creep of the snowpack as a result of gravity, or the pressure of skiers and piste machines. All of these influences change the shape of the snow crystal, breaking and melting the fine filaments.

Studying snow and knowing intimately the history of each snow layer as it falls during the winter provide a mountain guide with the sort of knowledge required to assess the danger of avalanche on a variety of different slopes. A guide also has years of experience and knowledge of the slopes in summer and what sort of terrain is supporting the snow layers.

Even on piste the speed and heaviness of the snow can differ from moment to moment and from turn to turn. Skiers, like Eskimos, have developed a vast terminology to describe the different snow conditions they encounter. As you develop your awareness, you will begin to add descriptive words to fit your experiences. From 'bottomless light powder' to 'bullet-proof ice', from 'velvety spring snow' to 'slush', the vocabulary indicates the depth of knowledge that comes from experience. We cannot learn about snow and skiing from books. They can only point the way. Both can become real only through experience.

Begin noticing the differences every time you ski. Feel the texture and speed of the snow. During your stay in the mountains notice the effect of the sun on slopes with different aspects, the effect of the wind and changes in temperature. Get into the habit of reading the snow. Look at the crystals. How cohesive is it? Is there enough humidity to make a snowball?

You can begin to assess how old the snow is and perhaps reflect on its past and future. This frozen droplet of moisture was once a part of an ocean that was sucked upwards, transformed into a cloud, travelled in the sky, frozen, and eventually fell with zillions of others, to be picked up by you and examined, skied on, melted by the spring sunshine or perhaps even remain stranded for decades high on a hanging glacier before returning to the sea, to source. The cycle of death and rebirth and the law of what goes up must come down are reflected even in the humble snowflake.

In exploring the nature of snow we develop a respect for its potency and the miracle of nature which provides us with such a wonderful playground.

PAYING RESPECTS

I went skiing this morning on Europe's greatest lift – serviced glacier, the Grand Montets above Argentière in the Mont Blanc massif. There are no piste machines on this mountain and only two marked runs. The rest is an off-piste paradise with spectacular seracs and yawning crevasses. Not a place I would recommend without a guide. I have been skiing here for several years and regard it as my playground – albeit a dangerous one.

Mid-April, fresh powder snow and the crowds of tourists had vanished - hopefully not down the crevasses. With hat, goggles and a pair of 203 cm giant slalom skis I was more than ready to join a couple of friends. My mind, always eager to proffer advice, began chipping in with comments about how it was quite a few days since I had skied and that at my age I should be careful. The visibility was variable and I should watch out for the heavier snow . . . here we go again, I observed. Doesn't one ever win the game of taming the mind? Apparently not, but even if one never wins, watching its antics and focusing on something more useful is the only game worth playing. So, thanking my mind for the warnings of which I was well aware, I put the worries in an imaginary rubbish bin. To disengage the effects of negativity, I asked myself, 'How would I ski this if I was 25 and fit?' and paid attention to my breathing.

We paid our respects to the virgin snow in the only way we know how, by taking the most direct and harmonious line and enjoying nature's gift of snow billowing over our heads. It was one of those days made even more wonderful by the need to stay alert. The clouds had their own plans, blowing in and out, changing the visibility and the nature of the game. The intermittent sunshine had its way with the settling snow on the lower slopes, changing the light flakes into heavier foot-grabbing crud.

After skiing 7,200 m (24,000 ft) in three hours I began to tire. Clearly, writing a book does nothing for the legs. So here I am, back at the word processor, reflecting on my experience this morning.

If we are to fully express our potential as human beings we need to be able to operate in a whole-brained way – to access our intuition and wisdom and use our intellect in a detached yet purposeful manner. If the mind is the inhibitor both off and on the slopes, then a fuller understanding of the mind is required. If the skier is other than the mind – then who is doing the skiing? We may ask these questions and look outside for the answers – the fishmonger will no doubt shop around – the fisherman will ask within, finding the truth by going beyond the mind.

When someone skis harmoniously down a mountain, a particular quality emerges and the only word that I can find to describe this is – grace. On the surface, skiing with grace manifests as a flowing and effortless dance with the terrain. Grace cannot be calibrated, analyzed and dissected. Grace is wholeness, completeness, balance personified. However grace may manifest externally, it is only a reflection of an inner attitude. Internally, there is clarity and surrender; detachment, respect and a trust in the body's ability to match the demands of the slope.

The awareness exercises in this book are ways to get beyond the mind and to find the serenity and joy in letting go and finding grace.

When I recall all the people who have guided me in my growth, they have a common quality that made more sense than anything they may have said or done: a knowing twinkle in their eyes, a playful lightness and spontaneous humour demonstrating that they knew life was just a game. If you are going to coach yourself successfully, remember skiing *is* only a game. When you get intense and things seem to be 'important', watch out. Your mind is finding a foothold. Let go, let it flow.

As Richard Bach says in *Illusions*, 'everything in this book may be wrong.' Do not fall into the trap of believing anything you read: find out what is true for you through your own experience.

**ENJOY SKIING. ENJOY THE MOUNTAINS.
ENJOY YOURSELF.**

RECOMMENDED FURTHER READING
SKIING

Abraham, Horst, *Skiing Right* (Johnson Books,) 1983.

Gallwey, Timothy & Kriegel, Bob, *Inner Skiing* (Random House,) 1977; (Pan Books) 1987.

Joubert, Georges, *Skiing, an Art........ a Technique* (Poudre Publishing,) 1978.

Loudis, Leonard, Lobitz, Charles, & Singer, Kenneth, *Skiing Out of Your Mind* (Springfield Books,) 1988.

Major, James & Larsson, Olle, *World Cup Ski Technique* (Poudre Publishing,) 1979.

McCluggage, Denise, *The Centered Skier* (Bantam,) 1973.

Shedden, John, *Skilful Skiing* (A. and C. Black,) 1982.

Shedden, John, *Skiing - Developing Your Skill* (The Crowood Press,) 1986.

GENERAL

Assagioli, Roberto, *Psychosynthesis* (Turnstone,) 1975.

Bach, Richard, *Illusions* (Pan Books,) 1977.

Bandler, Richard & Grindler, John, *Frogs into Princes* (Real People Press,) 1979.

Blakeslee, Thomas R., *The Right Brain* (Papermac,) 1980.

Buzan, Tony, *Use Your Head* (BBC Books,) 1982.

Castaneda, Carlos, *The Power of Silence* (Black Swan,) 1988.

Gallwey, Timothy, *The Inner Game of Tennis* (Cape,) 1975.

Gallwey, Timothy, *The Inner Game of Golf* (Cape,) 1979.

Gawain, Shakti, *Creative Visualisation* (Whatever Publishing,) 1978).

Millman, Dan, *The Warrior Athlete* (Stillpoint,) 1979.

Ornstein, Robert, *The Psychology of Consciousness* (Penguin,) 1972.

Ostrander, Sheila, & Schroeder, Lynn, *Superlearning* (Sphere Books,) 1981.

Rose, Colin, *Accelerated Learning* (Topaz,) 1985.

Shone, Ronald, *Creative Visualisation* (Thorsons,) 1984.

Stirk, John L. *Structural Fitness* (Elm Tree Books,) 1988.

Syer, John & Connelly, Christopher, *Sporting Body, Sporting Mind* (Cambridge University Press,) 1984. (Simon & Schuster,) 1987.

Tobias, Maxine, & Stewart, Mary, *Stretch and Relax* (Dorling Kindersley,) 1985.

Tobias, Maxine & Stewart, Mary, *The Yoga Book* (Pan Books,) 1986.

Whitmore, John, *The Winning Mind* (Fernhurst Books,) 1987.

INDEX